MOM,

Incorporated

MOM,
Incorporated

A GUIDE TO BUSINESS + BABY

Aliza Sherman and Danielle Elliott Smith

SELLERS
PUBLISHING

Aliza's Dedication

To my Renaissance-man husband and best friend, Gregory S. Risdahl.
I couldn't do what I do or be who I am without the light of your love.

To my daughter, Noa Grace. Your Mommy and Daddy love you very much, and now you
know what Mommy does when she's home on her computer.

Danielle's Dedication

To my husband, Jeff. You have made it possible for me to imagine a world where
I get to have a career I love and now, to live it. I couldn't have done it without you.

To my sweet and sassy small people, Delaney and Cooper — my life is better because of
you. And Delaney? THIS is why I didn't give up my phone and computer for Lent.

Published by Sellers Publishing, Inc.

Copyright © 2011 Aliza Sherman and Danielle Elliott Smith
All rights reserved.

Cover photo © Getty/Image Bank/Tara Moore

Sellers Publishing, Inc.
161 John Roberts Road, South Portland, Maine 04106
Visit our Web site: www.sellerspublishing.com • E-mail: rsp@rsvp.com

ISBN 13: 978-1-4162-0651-4
Library of Congress Control Number: 2011921887

10 9 8 7 6 5 4 3 2 1

Printed in United States of America.

Contents

Introduction

You're in the midst of another midnight feeding. You are struck by the quiet, the peace, the connection between you and your little one who is looking right at you. And then you suddenly hear a voice . . .

"There must be something more."

Who said that? Your eyes open wider. Your baby's eyes mirror yours as if to say, "I heard it, too."

You hear the voice again.

"There is something more."

Well, now you are starting to get a little nervous. You glance to the windows: closed. You listen past the sound machine: nothing. You push yourself from the rocking chair, at the risk of disrupting a peaceful feeding. Your husband? Still snoring.

But the voice sounds again. And this time you realize: it is the sound of your heart. Holding your baby in your arms, you are content, but there is a part of you that is searching for something else.

Something that belongs to just you.

You have no desire to return to the 9-to-5 grind working for someone else. You do want to be present for as many extraordinary moments in your child's life as possible. So what if you started your own business? What if you worked from home? How would you do it? Could you do it? Could you really find a way to handle it all?

Why, yes. Yes, you can.

This is a conversation you may be having with yourself while holding your baby in your arms. Or you may have small children at home when the idea for "something" hits you. Or you might be pregnant or planning to get pregnant and thinking a home-based business may create the ideal situation for yourself as a new mom. Your desire for "something more" may have been prompted by a life-changing event like it did for both of us — one of those moments that smacks you in the face and reminds you that life is short and that you need to live your dreams. Regardless of the reason, if you are having the urge to birth a new business and you have a baby or small children in the mix, this is the book for you.

As two moms who have successfully built our own home-based businesses while negotiating the landscape of motherhood, we have a passion for helping women like you to do the same. We've set out to provide you with the nitty-gritty details for starting a home-based business on your own — from how to tap into your passion and create the business you *want*, to the practical tips you *need* to get you started and keep you going even when you think you can't. There are moms who have managed to pull this off, many who admit to making mistakes along the way, but they did it. In this book, we bring some of their stories to you. We're certain many of the women's experiences shared within these pages will be inspiring to you.

Peppered throughout the book are some interactive quizzes to help you assess what you'll need moving forward, along with handy worksheets and checklists to give you step-by-step instructions for starting, running, and growing your business so you don't forget a thing. We've also proposed ideas about businesses that might be ideal for starting and running from home, particularly ones powered by the Internet. Let us help you avoid the missteps and move right to your life as a mom with a business.

You are Mom, Incorporated!

Danielle's story

A few years ago, I was floating through my days. I was happy as a mom, content that I was giving my kids all the attention and love they needed. But I knew my soul needed a little stirring. I ignored the voices inside encouraging me to pursue one dream or another until one Friday night in March 2007.

Driving home from my first "night out" after having my second child, my car was hit by a girl who ran a red light. I sped through the intersection, smacked a curb, and rolled down an embankment. I was conscious the entire time. I called my husband while I was hanging, nearly upside down, from my seat belt.

I walked away from that accident and into a "new" me. This new version of me vowed to listen to my inner voices, to respond to the soul stirrings, to start something of my very own. I decided I didn't want to work for anyone else — unless they were three foot three in fuzzy pajamas — and I wanted whatever I was doing to matter.

This was my passion coming up for air.

It was at that very moment that I decided to start ExtraordinaryMommy.com. My plans were vague. I knew I would be doing it all with my children right next to me. And that was good. I could be both mom and business owner. I knew there would be late hours. I knew it wouldn't be easy. But I knew I wanted it.

Now, chances are, you have the opportunity to listen to your "soul stirrings" without having to experience a released air bag and a totaled car. You don't need baseball-sized bruises and glass lodged in your hand to recognize the need to listen to your heart. You simply have to pay attention rather than hushing your inner voice and sending her back to her corner.

This experience, and my journey since then, taught me a few things:

- Listen to your soul stirrings — your heart will tell you if you are on the right path.
- Once you recognize that path, you have to CHOOSE to follow it. No one will do it for you.
- Put a plan in place. You may be tempted to "wing it," but your success will be dictated by that plan.
- There is no such thing as a "perfect balance" — and that is OK.
- You can do it. I have faith in you.

Let's see what your "Inner Mom, Incorporated" has to say . . .

Grab a pen and paper. Find a quiet corner — we know, a rarity in your world — but try. Settle in to listen to your heart, and allow us to lead you down the path to your personal passion. But first, listen to how Aliza ended up on her path.

Aliza's story

My business "birth story" is a little different from Danielle's, but I also started my first business after a life-changing event. I was held up at gunpoint and kidnapped with my boyfriend at the time. We were able to escape and later managed to catch the muggers and see them all go to jail, but the incident shook me to my core.

For me, staring down the barrel of a 9mm gun made me realize I didn't want to miss out on the chance to pursue my own dreams. I felt that working for someone else wasn't going to get me any closer to making something of my own. In 1995, I started an Internet company, Cybergrrl, Inc., with no money in the bank and nothing more than a great idea, a laptop, the Internet, and some hot pink business cards I made at Kinko's.

Fast-forward 12 years later. I had started my fifth company — a social media marketing agency — had great clients, and loved what I was doing each day. Then I had a baby. I wasn't prepared for the difficulties that would follow, including post-partum depression requiring medication. I had to put my business on hold — doctor's orders. I finally came out on the other side of these struggles, returned to running my business, and grew it with the help of a longtime friend. We brought on another business partner to help us expand it even more.

After over five years doing social media marketing, I decided I wanted to go solo again. I started another home-based venture in late 2010, a mobile apps development company, with my four-year-old daughter shuttling between pre-school, a babysitter's, and home. If I can complete four hours of work, I consider it a good day, and I try not to be jealous of my husband who works a full workday and gets so much done. But I wouldn't trade any of it because I love running my home-based business.

With my current business, I've learned from my past mistakes trying to manage clients, while a small child demanded my attention. My secret? Take on clients who get what it means to be a work-at-home-mom and respect and accept my situation. I'll never tell you that it's easy, but it can be done. The dynamics change every year as my daughter gets older, and they also change daily depending on the work at hand, the deadlines, the resources I have at my disposal, and even my mood and my daughter's mood. But on less productive or more frustrating days, I still don't regret my decision to leave a 9-to-5 workplace to become my own boss.

What have I learned after all of these years?

- Don't wait for something drastic or life-threatening to happen before you do what you love.

- Yes, you can start a business from home with a baby in your midst.

- Don't ever hesitate to ask for help.

- No, you can't do it all at once, but you can do it all, one thing at a time.

What do you want out of life and work? As Danielle said, let's see what your "Inner Mom, Incorporated" has to say . . .

Chapter 1
What Kind of Business Will You Grow?

What Makes You Tick?

This is your moment of truth. Are you ready to throw caution to the wind and pursue that dream, that BIG IDEA? What are you good at? What do you like to do? What do you want to create?

If you don't already have an idea for your business, the first two places to look can be your career up until this moment, and what else you've been doing. Many women who start businesses from home choose work related in some way to what they have done in the past. If you love what you've been doing and if it is something you're really good at — like creating beautiful jewelry or designing Web sites that make the savviest Internet user drool — then you could be on to something!

Starting a business based on your previous career could present a challenge — namely, your previous employer. Make sure there isn't a conflict and that you didn't sign a non-compete clause with them. If you did, having a heart-to-heart with your former boss and offering to be a consultant to the company so they can save on overhead could be an option. Or you may have to sit out that particular business idea for the duration of time stipulated in the non-compete document. Most non-compete clauses can be binding for somewhere between one to five years.

If your former career isn't a viable option for your new business, the second place to look for a business idea is what you do well or what you do every day. Do you know how to get kids to eat vegetables? Have you created a homing device for missing socks or mittens? Can you find absolutely anything on the Internet? Do you take amazing photographs of children? Make the BEST. FUDGE. EVER?

Can you create a business around that talent, hobby, or passion?

Why, of course you can.

Look at Johanna Parker of Kaya's Kloset. Before her daughter was born, she was an avid knitter. She'd knit her baby-to-be many things, including a ton of baby socks. She wanted her baby to only wear hand-knit socks. After her daughter was born, she quickly discovered — in the dead of winter — that hand-knit socks don't really stay on babies' feet. Realizing the knit socks weren't working, she sewed her baby girl a pair of baby shoes instead. The shoes fit, they stayed on, her baby's feet were covered, and — most important — were warm in the winter.

Johanna made a pair of shoes for a friend, then for some friends on the Internet, and finally set up a shop on Etsy, an online marketplace where you can both buy and sell handmade and vintage products.

She explains, "Etsy itself is a wonderful opportunity to allow businesses to start with very little start-up costs or efforts and grow at whatever pace works for the business owner. When I first opened my Etsy shop in June 2007, my daughter was only six months old. I only posted shoes that were in stock and didn't take custom orders."

Johanna continued to build her inventory slowly, and by that fall, she was able to participate in a few craft fairs, all with Kaya playing at her feet. As she grew more confident in her roles as business owner and mother, she was able to sew more, list more items on Etsy, participate in more craft fairs, and eventually build her own Web site apart from Etsy. Today, she attends fairs most weekends from May to December. She's also growing a wholesale business.

"It's more than a full-time job being a mom and a business owner," says Johanna. "But both are so incredibly fulfilling that I wouldn't give either up!"

Deciding to start a business from home is not like throwing a party for New Year's Eve. While both may happen in your comfort zone and both can be fun, only one is a true, long-term commitment. Knowing what to expect as you take the steps toward that commitment is essential.

You'll have fewer hiccups along the way as you start your business at home if you plan carefully. See Chapter 3 for guidance on writing down your actual business plan. Right now, we're just looking for your gut feelings and dreams.

So here's where the interactive part of this book starts. You can jot down a few notes here, or better yet, visit MomIncorporated.com to download printable worksheets, checklists, and brainstorming documents to get your creative juices flowing.

Write out your passions, talents, and skills:

What did you want to be "when you grew up"?

You used to be able to answer that question as a child, right? Consider yourself all grown up now. What do you want to be? Sometimes, even looking back at your childhood dreams can give you clues to what you're meant to be now.

What is your passion?

This is the part where you play smart. What do you love to do? Are you überorganized and love putting things in order? Are you so crafty that your friends are always asking you to decorate for the next party?

What are you good at?

These are concrete skills and talents you've nurtured. Did you manage to pick up on HTML like it was the language your parents used to speak to you when you were a child? Are you great at getting the word out about something?

Doesn't it feel great to write down aspects of yourself that you may not have explored in a long time? We hope it inspires you!

Which Type of Business Is Right for You?

While there are all kinds of businesses you can start, most people usually start one of four types of businesses. These four big categories help describe where a business is going to go and how it's going to grow.

Here is what we'd consider the four main types of business:

1. A Lifestyle Business. This is the business you start because you are motivated to have a certain lifestyle. You are looking for extra income or just enough to pay the bills. You want the freedom to make your own schedule, and you, quite simply, want to be in charge. But more than anything, the emphasis is on the lifestyle you want, often based on your passions. Melissa Lanz made just this decision when she started The Fresh 20, a healthy meal-planning service. Fed up with the number of times her family opted for takeout, she decided to make a change, starting a business that fit the lifestyle she wanted to lead. Her weekly healthy meal plans help thousands of customers to improve the way they eat. Her passion for good nutrition has grown to include the Family Food Summit, which brings together food industry leaders online to discuss healthy ways to feed families. She shares her journey on her blog, Soul on a Platter. Even as Melissa's business grows, she is living a life and building a business based on her passions, while raising her three boys.

2. An Income Business. This type of business requires more planning and potentially some outside help. You want this type of business because you seek to supplement your household income. For many women, this is the alternative to "heading back to work." There is a little more pressure involved in an Income Business than a Lifestyle Business because there is more at stake: the revenues are more integral to your household's well-being. As the recession impacted Amanda Moreno Duke's household and her husband's business was drastically affected, she realized she had next to nothing left to buy Christmas presents for her two young children. Out of her desire to provide for her family, her business — Cutie Pa Tutus — was born. She explains, "This was out of my bedroom, doing everything myself with a borrowed sewing machine. I sold enough to cover the expense of my supplies and still was able to contribute a couple hundred dollars that we couldn't afford otherwise towards Christmas presents." That Christmas? Her kids did not go without.

3. A Growing Business. If you are starting with either a Lifestyle or Income Business, you might end up with a Growing Business even if you didn't plan for it. There is a lot more pressure involved in a Growing Business, as your intention is just that — to grow and expand. With a Growing Business, you may eventually have to move your business out of your home — although you might still be able to work from home yourself while your team is in an office or workspace. Even if you are able to telecommute regularly, the demands on you will most likely be high. The pressure of starting a business with a more immediate growth strategy is that you will need to hire others more quickly, including building a strong sales force or business development team to meet larger sales goals. You will also have to make a greater initial investment of both time and money to catapult the business. Lisa Druxman of Stroller Strides started a business from an idea that combined her fitness industry background with her infant son's stroller: she incorporated her exercise routine into her daily schedule of taking him on walks and turned it into a class for new moms. Within a few years of teaching fitness classes to other moms with their babies in strollers, she brought on other instructors and began licensing her business idea out to other moms. Soon a franchise was born. Lisa later purchased a new house that included five built-in workstations, and hired twelve employees with keys, with the intent of continuing to run her business from home. Eventually, she did move her business out of her house and into a regular office. These days, Stroller Strides is one of the more affordable and fastest-growing franchises in the country.

4. A Go Big or Go Home Business. This is not typically the number-one choice for a mom looking to start something on her own from her home, as it requires a lot of everything — investment of time, money, and not just a desire but an ambitious, carefully calculated plan to grow quickly. This is also not the kind of business you can start solely on your own, as it requires the help of others and likely significant financial investments from outside sources to get off the ground.

Not everyone is cut out to Go Big or Go Home right out of the gate. In some cases, you might start one type of business and end up with another. For example, you might start a Lifestyle Business and end up with a Growing Business, like Melissa Lanz of The Fresh 20. Many of today's most successful businesses started by moms began initially out of a desire to stay home and "do something," but eventually grew to become major companies. A great example of this is Julie Aigner-Clark's business. She started out making homemade videos of her daughter's toys and began selling the videos. Her company expanded over a number of years to become Baby Einstein, and she eventually sold it to Disney!

Moms Know Best

Do a little more research first. I dove right in out of enthusiasm and motivation but you need to spend some time on research before spending any money on your new venture.

—Katie Newman, Gifts and Home

Danielle's business type

My business idea fell squarely in between a Lifestyle and an Income Business model. I knew I wanted additional income for our family, hoping to give my husband the freedom to choose a different, more enjoyable career path, but we weren't dependent on the money I would bring in. The "lifestyle" factor for me was the ability to set my own hours to be available for my kids — that was crucial to me. Picking the "right" business was important, not only for planning purposes but for my mindset. By knowing what I needed, by planning for the business that fit my life, I set myself up to succeed.

Aliza's business type

Each time I've started a new business, I've set out to have an Income Business, one that would pay the bills and then some. In several instances, those businesses turned into Growing Businesses because something caught on — a little bit of the right time/right place happening. More recently, I intentionally switched my six-figure Income Business into a Growing Business by bringing on a business partner (a trusted friend). When I moved to a rural area where childcare was scarce, I began to feel the strain of the larger business, so I took a less active role in the expanding company. I then started something smaller and more manageable. For a time, I thought I'd go for a Go Big or Go Home Business, but having less stress in my life won over.

Deciding what size business you want to have is a very personal choice, and there is no wrong decision if it is right for you.

Moms Know Best

Don't listen to ALL those people who will tell you that you don't have time to start a business at home. Your mother-in-law will tell you that you don't have time. Your neighbor, your sister, your child's friend's aunt, and your mail carrier will tell you that you're crazy. You are NOT crazy! You have a brain, a creative drive, and the spirit to do it, and you'll be just fine.

—Michelle Ciarlo-Hayes, MKC Photography

K.I.S.S. —
Keeping It Simple, Sister!

As you are rolling potential options around in your brain, consider the benefits of keeping it simple. A home-based sole proprietorship — a business you run all by yourself out of your home — is a good place to start. Another way to Keep It Simple, Sister is to choose a "service business" over a "products business." Here are some reasons why:

About a Service-Oriented Home-Based Business:

1. **Low overhead.** You are at home and not paying for office space.
2. **Less pressure.** You can make your own schedule and work in your pajamas if you want.
3. **No employees to worry about.** You may have a few off-site contractors, but they're independent, not dependent on you.
4. **Low equipment needs.** Usually specialized — and expensive — equipment comes into play when you have a products business.
5. **It's a more straightforward and less complex business.** Services businesses are very common and usually fairly easy to get started.

About a Product-Oriented Home-Based Business:

1. **High overhead.** While you can produce some products in your home, in many cases you need larger spaces and even special equipment.
2. **High cost of market research.** If you are going to invest in producing and marketing products, you need to do your homework, and that can be time-consuming and pricey.
3. **High cost of development.** Things like patents and prototypes are costs you don't usually see with a service business.
4. **Production costs and logistics.** Manufacturing on a large scale is costly, as is distributing and marketing your products.
5. **More complex type of business.** In general, you'll find having a products business requires more steps and more considerations than a service-oriented company.

If you want to start a products business, don't worry. There are some smart and cost-effective ways to sell your products online, and we cover some of those options in Chapter 2.

Time After Time

Before you start singing the Cyndi Lauper song to yourself, let's clear up the misperception that you have all sorts of time to make your business dream a reality. Now is the time to sit down and map that out. When will you get things done?

Maybe that little angel of yours sleeps a lot, but when you tally her naps, she probably only sleeps for about an hour and a half in the morning and two hours in the afternoon. Will three-and-a-half hours be enough time for you to start and run your brand-new business?

This is the moment when you realize that there are, in fact, only 24 hours in a day, and you are required to sleep, eat, and take care of your family during some of them. Before you get discouraged, here are a few questions you should answer to find the time you need.

WORKSHEET: Getting a Handle on Time

You can also download this worksheet at MomIncorporated.com.

What days of the week would you like to work?	
What times of day are you planning to dedicate to this new endeavor?	
How will you be able to get work done with a baby or kids around?	
How many hours a week will it take for you to start this business? *(See Chapter 3, where we walk you through creating a business plan and other initial steps for setting up your business.)*	

Amee Quiriconi started her business, Squak Mountain Stone, in 2003, when her son was just a toddler. She actually invented a way to make countertops out of recycled materials. This type of business was labor intensive and required time to research the market. Her new business also depended on a large space where she could work. How did she find — or make — the time to work on her business with a child around? She first made sure that her workspace was always safe and conducive for her son — and later her daughter — to be with her while she worked.

She explains, "My kids never touched or were near any of the raw materials, which are just dusty. But what was always present in my mind were the other hazards that existed in the shop, such as a forklift." So, Amee was always clear with everyone that safety was paramount: "I imparted a high level of safety consciousness with my employees, reminding them that they needed to be vigilant with their actions, not only for their own well-being but also for that of my kids when they were around.

"My kids never have free rein around the shop, but one can't assume that, when you leave your office to go out and answer a question for one of your employees, your little ones will stay put."

She also found that including her children in her work was her best option.

"I engaged my son in my business," says Amee. "He has my engineering mind, and it was easier to work with him there when I was able to let him 'help' around the shop, even at three and four years old."

Amee taught her son how to put the stickers on her samples and how to perform other small, easy, and safe tasks. You, too, may opt to include your kids in your business, if feasible, or to work around your family's schedule.

Lisa Lehmann focuses her passion on two things: her family and her jewelry business. She created Studio Jewel in 2001, and it has always been a family affair. She recognizes that her schedule is a bit unconventional, but it works: "I work on Saturdays. My boundaries are clear. They may look different than those of other families, but it is a balance game."

Part of that balance now means that her oldest daughter, Anneke, age 14, actually works for her — giving them extra time together.

"Anneke has always helped to some degree. Now she does all my finish work. Wire work. Drilling holes. Cutting disks. Getting everything ready to solder. I just pass things along and say 'do this' and it's done . . . and done well."

Just this year, Lisa started paying her daughter for her hard work — truly making it worth her effort.

"This is a big commitment," says Lisa. "I don't do this because Mommy wants to be busy, but because Mommy needs to do this. My family needs to be aware of the sacrifices. I feel it is so valuable for them to learn an actual skill and be a part of what makes their mama so crazy busy!"

Carissa Brown, founder of the Carissa Rose clothing line, always tried to include her children as much as possible in her business as well.

"I have paid my children a nickel or dime for every catalog they stuffed, mailer they stamped, tag they stickered, etc.," says Carissa. "I gave the older ones challenges, too. My nine-year-old could pretty much ship anything I asked him to."

Danielle's schedule

On more than one occasion, my husband has accused me of being nocturnal. I have been known to work until 2:00 and 3:00 a.m. — that's often when I do my very best work. I'm the kind of girl who needs to back her way into creativity. It is impossible for me to flip a creative switch that allows me to start producing stellar work. I'm especially prone to distraction if I know someone might need me. And if anyone in the house is awake, interruption becomes more likely, so my productivity on labor-intensive projects during the day is suspect.

And I'm not alone. We moms are a resourceful bunch, and we know we can't subsist on a mere three hours of sleep a night. We find a way to make it work. But finding a schedule that works isn't always easy. I will forever admit that my schedule is a work-in-progress — and it has to be: I'm a mom. I work from home. This means my priorities occasionally shift from a planned day of conference calls, writing, projects, and meetings to one of nursing a small person through a 103-degree fever. And don't even get me started on snow days!

Aliza's schedule

I can't work in the wee hours of the night or early morning. By 4:00 p.m., I'm mentally exhausted. There never seems to be enough time in the day to get everything done, but I've learned to accept that is just the nature of the beast.

My husband has really emphasized how important it is to him that we put our work aside in the evenings, have dinner together as a family, and unwind and spend time together before bedtime. He doesn't like it when I pull my laptop out for a quick peek at the e-mails I didn't get to earlier in the day. When I'm feeling over-loaded, I carve out time on weekends, prearranging it with my husband, and if he wants to get something done, I occasionally can find a babysitter to help out with my daughter. Sometimes, I try to wake up an hour or two earlier than my husband

and daughter, to get in some quiet productive time. And when I occasionally wake up in the middle of the night, plagued with that nagging feeling that I forgot to do something, I may sneak out of bed to work for a while by the glow of my laptop, but I try not to make a habit of that.

Like Danielle said, we moms are a resourceful bunch!

The important question you need to answer isn't simply, "when is the best time to work?" but "when is the best time for you to work?"

Go to MomIncorporated.com to download the calendar template and sample calendar schedule on the following pages, as well as the worksheet to "Find Your Missing Time."

Take naps during the day and learn to get work done on off-hours. You'd be surprised how alert and sharp you can be at 3:00 a.m. if you've had a good nap the day before. Your clients won't have any idea (or care) when you did the work, as long as you get it done on time!

—Natasha Biasell, Ivy Public Relations

"I Can Do Whatever I Want"

Starting a business means you can do whatever you want, right? Well . . . yes and no.

Right now, you might have stars in your eyes and are thinking that having your own business simply means being your own boss, not having to answer to anyone, and having lots of flexibility. You are practically giddy with the thought of making your own schedule. But let us break it down for you.

You can be your own boss. You don't answer to anyone.

But you *do* have to answer to yourself. And your clients or customers. And also to the family that is supporting you on your quest to start your own business. That responsibility is a pretty big one.

SAMPLE DOC: Weekly Calendar Template

You can use this blank calendar sheet to find your pockets of work time interspersed with the rest of your life, or use a free, handy online calendaring system such as Google Calendar. You can find links to free, printable calendar sheets on MomIncorporated.com.

	Sunday	Monday	Tuesday	Wednesday	Thursday	Friday	Saturday
6:00 am							
6:15 am							
6:30 am							
6:45 am							
7:00 am							
7:15 am							
7:30 am							
7:45 am							
8:00 am							
8:15 am							
8:30 am							
8:45 am							
9:00 am							
9:15 am							
9:30 am							
9:45 am							
10:00 am							
10:15 am							
10:30 am							
10:45 am							
11:00 am							
11:15 am							
11:30 am							
11:45 am							
12:00 pm							
12:15 pm							

	Sunday	Monday	Tuesday	Wednesday	Thursday	Friday	Saturday
12:30 pm							
12:45 pm							
1:00 pm							
1:15 pm							
1:30 pm							
1:45 pm							
2:00 pm							
2:15 pm							
2:30 pm							
2:45 pm							
3:00 pm							
3:15 pm							
3:30 pm							
3:45 pm							
4:00 pm							
4:15 pm							
4:30 pm							
4:45 pm							
5:00 pm							
5:15 pm							
5:30 pm							
5:45 pm							
6:00 pm							
6:15 pm							
6:30 pm							
6:45 pm							
7:00 pm							
7:15 pm							
7:30 pm							
7:45 pm							
8:00 pm							

SAMPLE DOC: Danielle's Typical Weekly Schedule

Here's a "real life" example of how a weekly schedule might look, but keep in mind that things don't always stick to schedule or go as planned!

	Sunday	Monday	Tuesday	Wednesday	Thursday	Friday	Saturday
6:00 am		Wake up	Wake up	Wake up	Wake up	Wake up	
6:15 am		Get kids up for school	Get kids up for school	Get kids up for school	Get kids up for school	Get kids up for school	
6:30 am		Get kids fed and ready for school	Get kids fed and ready for school	Get kids fed and ready for school	Get kids fed and ready for school	Get kids fed and ready for school	
6:45 am							
7:00 am							
7:15 am		↓	↓	↓	↓	↓	
7:30 am		School drop-off	School drop-off	School drop-off	School drop-off	School drop-off	
7:45 am							
8:00 am		Gym	Gym	Gym	Gym	Gym	
8:15 am							
8:30 am							
8:45 am							
9:00 am		↓	↓	↓	↓	↓	
9:15 am							
9:30 am							
9:45 am							
10:00 am		Social media	Social media	Social media	Social media	Social media	
10:15 am							
10:30 am							
10:45 am							
11:00 am							
11:15 am							
11:30 am							
11:45 am		↓	↓	↓	↓	↓	
12:00 pm		Lunch	Lunch	Lunch	Lunch	Lunch	
12:15 pm		↓	↓	↓	↓	↓	
12:30 pm		Calls, writing, projects	Calls, writing, projects	Calls, writing, projects	Calls, writing, projects	Calls, writing, projects	
12:45 pm		↓	↓	↓	↓	↓	

	Sunday	Monday	Tuesday	Wednesday	Thursday	Friday	Saturday
1:00 pm		Calls, writing, projects	Calls, writing, projects	Calls, writing, projects	Calls, writing, projects	Calls, writing, projects	
1:15 pm							
1:30 pm							
1:45 pm							
2:00 pm							
2:15 pm							
2:30 pm							
2:45 pm							
3:00 pm							
3:15 pm		↓	↓	↓	↓	↓	
3:30 pm		Kids home from school	Kids home from school	Kids home from school	Kids home from school	Kids home from school	
3:45 pm		Kids' homework	Kids' homework	Kids' homework	Kids' homework	Kids' homework	
4:00 pm							
4:15 pm		↓	↓	↓	↓	↓	
4:30 pm		Quality time w/kids	Quality time w/kids	Quality time w/kids	Quality time w/kids	Quality time w/kids	
4:45 pm							
5:00 pm							
5:15 pm		↓	↓	↓	↓	↓	
5:30 pm		Dinner	Dinner	Dinner	Dinner	Dinner	
5:45 pm							
6:00 pm							
6:15 pm		↓	↓	↓	↓	↓	
6:30 pm			Soccer/T-ball practice and games	Soccer/T-ball practice and games	Soccer/T-ball practice and games		
6:45 pm							
7:00 pm							
7:15 pm							
7:30 pm							
7:45 pm			↓	↓	↓		
8:00 pm		Kids' baths, reading	Kids' baths, reading	Kids' baths, reading	Kids' baths, reading	Kids' baths, reading	
8:15 pm		↓	↓	↓	↓	↓	
8:30 pm		Kids' bedtime	Kids' bedtime	Kids' bedtime	Kids' bedtime	Kids' bedtime	
8:45 pm		Work until 1 am	Work until 1 am	Work until 1 am	Work until 1 am	Work until 1 am	

Danielle's view

One of the reasons I started my own business was to have full control of my own schedule. I didn't want to answer to someone else. I have the flexibility to work around the important moments in my life. I can say yes or no to potential projects and clients based on the life I want to lead. I don't miss soccer games or holiday pageants. But it does mean I've missed out on more than a few precious hours of sleep to make up for it. Take, for example, the writing of this book. I can promise you, I'm not only writing during daylight hours.

Aliza's view

I must confess that I, too, love the flexibility of having my own business. Having started and run both sole proprietorships and even larger companies with anywhere from half a dozen to several dozen team members, I've seen both sides. I must admit that I get antsy and frustrated in a more structured environment. Being my own boss and setting my own schedule, as well as not having to worry about the livelihood of lots of other people, works best for me.

While you can do whatever you want, if you are looking to operate a business successfully, you will have to create a schedule for yourself. And more important, you need to stick to it. We hear that the boss can be a bear, even if the boss is you.

Do You Want a "Jobbie" or a "Hobby"

We are assuming you want to make some money with your entrepreneurial endeavor. Don't we all? This isn't going to be a hobby that might make you a little cash on the side. Entrepreneur and business advisor Carol Roth calls that a "jobbie," not a business.

As Carol explains it, many women have "jobbies" or a hobby disguised as a job or business.

"These part-time endeavors can be excellent ways to explore passions, test out the viability of a business, and make some side money," says Carol. "But women — and men for that matter, too — can get tricked by a jobbie to the point they are wrapped up thinking they have a full-fledged business and spend too much time, money, and effort on something that will never get to the next level."

She continues, "One of the key differentiations is deciding if you are 'me-centric' or 'customer-centric.' In today's business environment, a successful business is all about servicing customers. On the other hand, hobbies are about indulging your wants. If you want to have a true business, you need to put the customer first. If you are leading with your own needs (fulfilling your passion, your creativity, you, you, you!), then you may be better suited for a hobby."

The most important thing to remember is that it doesn't matter if you want a business or a jobbie.

"What matters is that you make a decision," Carol explains. "You can't decide the best path to get somewhere if you don't know where it is you are going."

Whether big or small, we understand that you want to create something of your very own that will provide you with a steady income or help you contribute to your household income, affording you the opportunity to work on something you love while you stay home with your kids. Call it what you want, just know what it is you're going after. If you're going after the money, then own it!

Repeat after us: "I want a profitable business."

Only you can decide if you are looking for "fun money" — money to take your family on trips or buy some of the things you have always wanted — or to contribute a significant amount to your current household income. Or maybe you want to become the sole household breadwinner to allow your partner to pursue a dream. Figure this out now, because it will affect everything — from the type of business you will start to how you will go about building it. Keep in mind, however, that your personal — and professional — needs can change over time, including if you have more children or if your children are no longer at home but are off to school.

If you're still in the planning stages for starting your family as you also start your business, expect major changes once you do have a baby. Anticipate a lull in revenues from your business if all income generation relies on your efforts. In the case of moms-to-be, starting a service business may require that you bring in some temporary help while you're in the throes of the world of a newborn. If you have a products company, you may want to produce extra product to have sufficient inventory until you're back to a regular production schedule. Or you may simply want to prepare for the reduced income during this time.

Danielle on money

When I first decided to start my own business, my financial planning was vague. "Vague" is the word I use, but I'm being kind. This is where you get to learn from my mistakes. I actually said to myself, "By the time Cooper (my youngest child) is in school full time, I would like to be a financial contributor to my family."

In my head I knew that meant I wanted to take over a large portion of our bills so that my husband could pursue a job he enjoyed. Also tied up in that was my desire to feel like a "contributor." As a woman who didn't get married until she was thirty, I had plenty of experience taking care of myself and paying my own bills. It felt odd to no longer see a paycheck with my name on it.

When I started my business, I never came up with an actual number in my head, and I never wrote one down. That was a mistake.

I now know my financial goals include:

- Being responsible for some of our household expenses.
- Creating a financial cushion that allows my husband the mental freedom to seek out a career he enjoys instead of one he feels obligated to do.
- Having money set aside to allow our family to "splurge" on vacations and experiences.

Write down your number. It might not be the right number, but you have to start somewhere.

Aliza on money

I've always started businesses thinking, "If I can just make enough to pay the bills," but over the years, I've learned that isn't good enough. When I brought on a business partner for my last company, I was grateful for her incredible business savvy, because she helped me see that the numbers in my head — if I even could come up with any — were small potatoes. In the first quarter after she joined me, she tripled the company's revenues.

These days, I'm back on my own, and I find myself struggling again with thinking too small. Yet I know that I want three specific things out of this business:

- To eliminate our household debt.
- To be able to save for retirement and actually have a savings account with money in it.
- To afford to travel with my family without a trip putting us deep in the hole and stressing us out.

So I've come up with numbers that will help me not just meet these goals but surpass them.

Debra M. Cohen, founder of Home Remedies of NY, Inc., left Corporate America and initially wanted to contribute a few hundred dollars a month to her household income, so her family could afford her staying at home full time with an infant daughter.

"As my business grew over time, I set bigger and bigger goals for myself," says Debra. "First, I wanted to make enough money to pay for my daughter's gymnastics class. Then, I was making enough money to pay for a cleaning lady and a gardener every week. Eventually, my business started to generate enough income for me to save enough to renovate our home and even save for college."

What does Debra feel helped her business grow? She cites her husband's unwavering support and a $5,000 loan from their retirement savings as two big boosts to growth.

How much money do you want or need to make? And when would you like to start seeing a profit or a significant impact from what you bring in? Write it down now.

I want to make (realistically, of course, because we all want to make a million, right?):	$
I need to make (what do you think you need to make — guesstimate):	$
I want to start seeing a profit by (how long do you think it will take you? Make a quick guess.):	

Once you begin filling out the next budget sheet, you'll find that this first exercise may show you that sometimes the numbers we think we want or need to make don't necessarily match up to real numbers based on our current household income, expenses, and expectations. Don't worry if your numbers are far off — this is an important lesson for us all to learn.

Never doubt your abilities, as a mother or as a professional!

—Jean Guerriero, Big City Dogs

BUDGET SHEET: Use this to write down your current household expenses.

The following sheet can help you figure out roughly how much it costs to run your household, how much your spouse or partner can contribute, and a general estimate of the amount of income your new business would need to generate for you to make a minimum contribution. Later, you will have to add your business expenses to the picture, to understand how much more you'll have to make to cover those as well.

Household Expenses	Monthly Cost Estimate	% of Expense Your Spouse or Partner Can Cover	Monthly Amount You Need to Help Cover	6 Months Household Expenses You Need to Help Cover	12 Months Household Expenses You Need to Help Cover
Ex: Mortgage	$1,000.00	100%	$0.00	$0.00	$0.00
Ex: Utilities/Phone	$250.00	100%	$0.00	$0.00	$0.00
Ex: Groceries	$800.00	50%	$400.00	$2,400.00	$4,800.00
Ex: Living & Entertainment	$250.00	50%	$125.00	$750.00	$1500.00
Ex: Slush Fund for Unexpected	$500.00	100%	$0.00	$0.00	$0.00
TOTAL	$2,800.00		$525.00	$3,150.00	$6,300.00
	This is how much it costs at a minimum to run your household each month.		This is the minimum amount you would need to generate with your business each month to contribute to your household income.	This is the minimum amount you would need to generate with your business over the first 6 months to contribute.	This is the minimum amount you would need to generate with your business over the first year to contribute.

Now it's your turn. Remember that these sheets are available for download on MomIncorporated.com.

Household Expenses	Monthly Cost Estimate	% of Expense Your Spouse or Partner Can Cover	Monthly Amount You Need to Help Cover	6 Months Household Expenses You Need to Help Cover	12 Months Household Expenses You Need to Help Cover
Ex: Mortgage	$	%	$	$	$
Ex: Utilities/ Phone	$	%	$	$	$
Ex: Groceries	$	%	$	$	$
Ex: Living & Entertainment	$	%	$	$	$
Ex: Slush Fund for Unexpected	$	%	$	$	$
	$	%	$	$	$
	$	%	$	$	$
	$	%	$	$	$
	$	%	$	$	$
	$	%	$	$	$
	$	%	$	$	$
	$	%	$	$	$
	$	%	$	$	$
	$	%	$	$	$
	$	%	$	$	$
	$	%	$	$	$
	$	%	$	$	$
	$	%	$	$	$
	$	%	$	$	$
TOTAL	$		$	$	$

Knowing what you need to make helps you understand how much you have to sell or charge for your products or services to cover expenses — and hopefully make real money! This worksheet is just meant to give you a picture of some immediate expenses that can impact decisions about the business you want to start.

The Balance Between Work and Life

We've talked about time issues and money issues, but what about those elusive "balance" issues? Right now, you might be waiting for us to swing down from the heavens with the SECRET to Work/Life Balance.

So here it is . . .

Our Balance (READ: PEACEFUL) Wisdom:

There is no such thing as perfect balance —
and the sooner you embrace that fact,
the more balanced you will feel.

Some days, some hours, some minutes, you will be a STELLAR Mom. And other days, hours and minutes, you will EXCEL as a Business Owner. You will rarely, if ever, be extraordinary at both at the very same time. Why? It is impossible to read your child her favorite story, help with homework, or cheer at a soccer game at the same time as you are answering a client call, responding to an e-mail, or writing a press release. Something has got to give.

And, THAT IS OK. *Say it with us:* **THAT IS OK.**

You need to set aside time for work and time for family — and don't forget the time you need to set aside for yourself. Will things always line up according to your plans? No, most likely not. But having a plan in place can help you to feel a little more sane and in control.

Danielle on balance

For the longest time, the word "balance" felt like a bad word to me. I was certain there was a secret handshake — a code word even — that allowed only the most special of mothers into the mythical world of balance. I was certain if I could just be strong enough, smart enough, organized enough, I would crack the code. But it wasn't happening. And the only success I saw was the successful failure to balance my work and home lives. Until one day it hit me: Balance is impossible.

Balance is a myth. At least, based on the definition we were being fed by society. It was — and it IS — impossible for me to be everything to everyone, every day. So I stopped trying. And I realized that giving my family my full attention when I am with them is the most important thing I can do. And giving my work my greatest effort when I'm in business mode is also important. So now, I'm at peace. Most of the time.

CHEAT SHEET: 10 Tips to Keep You Feeling Peaceful

1. **Prioritize.** It sounds silly, right? But it MATTERS. If you don't know what you HAVE to do, you will end the day feeling as though you failed, and that is definitely not a peaceful feeling.

2. **Only wear one hat at a time.** When you work, work. Don't fill out permission slips and try to help with homework. When you're wearing your "mom" hat and making dinner, don't stop to answer e-mails or tweet from your phone. You will actually feel your heart begin to race when you try to be too many things to too many people at once.

3. **Set clear work hours.** Let your clients know you are available for calls between 8:30 a.m. to 2:00 p.m. on Tuesdays and Thursdays and from noon to 2:00 p.m. on Mondays. Be specific. Stick with it, and make sure they do, too.

4. **Set boundaries.** Know your limits. Not just what you can and can't do in every area of your life but also, as important, what you are WILLING to do.

5. **Commit to something that matters to you and your family.** Maybe you promise to eat dinner as a family, have a game night, or some other family-only activity. Make sure you do it regularly, no excuses. Be someone your family can count on.

6. **Embrace the emotions that come with being a working mom.** Sometimes you will feel guilty, and that is OK. Since you are fully present when you are committed to be, know that your guilt is fleeting.

7. **Schedule time for you.** Whether it's reading, exercise, scrapbooking, sewing, or a pedicure, do SOMETHING that reminds you of who YOU are.

8. **Plan time with your girlfriends.** You know those people who make you laugh until you cry? The ones who will watch the sappy movies with you and understand your need to listen to the New Kids on the Block? You need some of them in your life to help you blow off steam.

9. **Get quiet time.** Find some. Make some. Have some. Your mind and spirit need it — even 15 minutes a day to JUST BE. This allows you to center, refresh, and refocus.

10. **Go for PEACE.** You don't have to use the word "balance." It makes your heart ache even THINKING about it, right? It is a bar someone has placed just out of your reach. Instead, know that you are simply seeking peace.

Aliza on balance

I've pretty much thrown the word — and concept — of "balance" out the window. I prefer to refer to it as a "juggle," as in "work/life juggle." To me, juggling is a perfect analogy for having to toggle back and forth between family and clients, between housework and project work. Like the expression "having many plates in the air," I feel that you can only juggle so many things before you drop something.

So the way I handle the "work/life juggle" is to pay close attention to what I'm juggling and to keep the number of things I juggle down to a manageable size. I keep rechecking my To Do list not just to see what I've been able to do and what is still outstanding, but also to look deeper and ask myself, "Am I overcommitting myself?"

If you know anything about being a type A overachiever, you know how hard it is to say "no" to requests or to admit you can't do something. Trust me, if you say "no" more often and reduce the number of plates you have to keep in the air, you'll get more done with less stress.

I also like the way Danielle talks about putting full attention to family when she is with her family and full attention to work when she is in work mode. That is something I've been working hard on because I know that my mind is not at its peak performance when divided between work and family. Even if you are a master at multitasking, you aren't really doing your absolute best when your attention is broken down to serve many things at once.

Moms Know Best

The only way I ever feel any sense of balance at all is by embracing the chaotic imbalance that is motherhood. Just acceptance, I guess, that I can't be and do it all and that's OK. I can do a lot of things well, and when I relax into imbalance, I usually end up getting more done . . . more peacefully.

—Heather Westberg King, author of *The Extraordinary Ordinary*

Getting Past the Guilt

Sometimes dinner won't be on the table on time. Sometimes you will forget it is "dress-down" day at your child's school — and your son or daughter will be THE ONLY ONE in uniform. Sometimes you do have to forgo a family outing to finish a client project (or edit a book). Sometimes the world seems to conspire to make you feel guilty because you are in the process of trying to do it all. The important thing to remember is that your kids do know you love them. The burned spaghetti won't convince them otherwise. They might resort to asking for Dad to cook every once in a while, but that wouldn't be all bad, now would it?

You need to remember to keep things in perspective.

"Unless you're saving lives, it really IS okay if work has to wait a few hours or even a day," says Cara Schrock, who owns the online baby products store, UrbanBabyRunway. com. "Missing your child's first words just because you think the world will end if So-and-So doesn't receive their T-shirt in three days instead of four isn't worth it."

Schrock adds that it is OK if your child has to play quietly alone for three minutes instead of whining and trying to interrupt you while you make a quick call to a customer. There is always something to feel guilty about. We say: Just. Don't. Do. It.

Dealing with an Identity Crisis

Before you decided to take this wild business-starting ride, you already wore at least a few hats: mom, wife, daughter, friend, maybe sister, perhaps even community volunteer or activist. But this new role, this whole "business owner" thing, has you feeling overwhelmed. Who are you anyway?

Aliza on identity

While it is still painful to admit, I was so into my career through my twenties and thirties and then spent several years trying to have a baby that when I finally did, I wasn't sure anymore *why* I wanted to be a mom. I just wanted to return to working on my business. Being a mom seemed so foreign to me, and starting a business was so familiar.

My struggle to be comfortable in my mommy role spanned several years. It wasn't until my daughter started talking — and I could finally understand what she needed — that I felt my mommy role was becoming a more manageable one. Instead of worrying about how to be a mom, which I finally understand is a continuous learning experience, I just feel good about adding "mother" to my many other roles.

Danielle on identity

If you had spoken to me when I was in my early twenties, I would have told you two things:

1. I wanted to have children when I was "young" — I was still thinking twenties. I'd always had a good relationship with my mom and dad, and they were 21 and 23, respectively, when they had me, so I figured that was the way to go.
2. I had NO INTENTION of being at home with my kids. I had chosen a career, and I was sticking with it.

Funny, neither of these things happened. I was over 30 when I had my daughter, and I was so instantly smitten with her that I did choose to "stay home," believing that was the right decision for my family. This choice did give me a bit of an identity crisis. I felt called to do something "more," and that is what led me to start my own business. Of course, that still means wearing many hats and "juggling," as Aliza calls it.

Giving Yourself a Break

How else are you going to get through the day-to-day, the chaos, the juggle, avoid the guilt, and do well in your roles? You've heard the adage that if you don't take care of yourself, no one else will. Well, take that to heart, because unless you take some time for yourself, you won't be good to anyone, and your relationships — and your business — will suffer. You need to come first. When you're happy and healthy, anything is possible.

"Be realistic with yourself and kind to yourself if you are running a business and taking care of a baby," says Niki Lopez, owner of Focus Marketing and PR. "The house won't always be clean, and dinner won't always be made. But if you are happy and fulfilled with your situation, then you are doing the right thing at the right time." Don't worry — running a business doesn't mean your family will go hungry! This is when leftovers, frozen meals, or even takeout can come in handy.

Danielle on self-care

At a particularly low point in my pseudo "balanced" career and life, I had a conversation with my family doctor, who also happens to be a friend. She was able to be brutally honest with me. I confessed to feeling completely off-kilter — unable to "right" myself. I was concerned I was failing in the great game of "Life Balance."

She brought me back to reality with this analogy: "Moms are a lot like boats. Like a boat, if a mom gets a 'hole' and refuses to address the problem or plug the leak, she will eventually bring everyone on the boat down with her."

That was when I realized that my ability to take care of myself was of utmost importance to my family. This meant I had to let go of my need to be everything to everyone at all times.

Aliza on self-care

Whenever I feel stressed out that I'm not doing enough or not doing things well, I keep reminding myself that "I'm doing the best I can right now." My family is happy, healthy, and loved. My business is thriving. I love doing the work that I do. And if I miss a deadline by a day or two, the world doesn't come to an end. Wow, imagine that. I know I do my best at each thing I do in my work and in my life when I'm well rested, healthy, and under minimal stress.

What are some things you can do to put yourself first without the guilt? Carve out time for yourself each day, whether you get up sooner or stay up later. We also recommend practicing meditation — we're not kidding. As little as 15 minutes a day can provide you time to refocus and refresh. Just take care of you. Eat well, drink plenty of water, exercise even if for just 20 minutes each day. You can't be your best or the best mom or the best business owner if you aren't healthy. For "Five Creative Ways to Learn to Put Yourself First," visit MomIncorporated.com.

You've come this far. Well done! By now we've given you food for thought to:

- Identify your passions, interests, and skills.
- Think about how to make your time work for you.
- Outline your basic financial needs to start to understand how much money you want to make with your business.
- Consider the work/life balance in a more realistic way.
- Start addressing the emotional aspects of starting a business, not just looking at the business side.

A few baby steps down, but many more to go. One step at a time.

Chapter 2
Tapping the Power of the Internet

The Internet provides both professionals and business owners with unprecedented access to information, resources, work-related tools, promotional tools, and customers. Personally, we love the Internet and what it offers us for our work and our lives. So why not consider starting a Web-based business or a business that can be bolstered by ongoing use of the Web? It makes a lot of sense, especially if you already have a computer, computer skills, and a good Internet connection, and you can find a business that matches your interests and skills.

If you have a baby or small children at home, and you want to stay home, we recommend that you start with a smaller, more compact business that requires a low capital investment; that is, less money down up-front. This recommendation also fits if you're currently pregnant or even planning for a family and considering a home-based business. We're not trying to discourage you from building an empire — far from it! But if the last thing you want is a stressful, highly demanding business that pulls you away from your family and home, you can make the choices that give you more control over your workload. And if you haven't given birth yet, any mom will tell you that once you have your baby, everything you ever thought you were going to do may not happen exactly as planned, to put it mildly.

All new businesses can be stressful, but you can keep the stress to a minimum by knowing your strengths, your limitations, your expectations, and your preferences. No amount of money is worth it if it generates stress. The costs of that stress can add up — affecting your business and, most important, taking a major toll on you in terms of increased healthcare costs, relationship costs, and even costs to your sanity.

If you are looking to start your first business from home, think about the right kind of business that meets the initial goals you set in Chapter 1. Then consider how leveraging the Web can provide a low-cost way to start a business with a high return for your efforts. While we think the businesses we're about to share with you can be fun, interesting, and challenging in some good ways, each one may also be demanding in its own way as well. Be realistic about what you're undertaking. Don't bite off more than you can chew. You know what we mean!

Don't take on a HUGE business idea if you have no help and small kids that are not even in preschool yet. Start small and build it up so that once they are off to school, you are already on your way.

—Christine, Simple Starfish

We Practice What We Preach

We both have businesses that are based predominantly online, so we're big fans of the Internet and what it has helped us achieve. Here's a little about our businesses and how the Web plays a significant part in what we do:

Danielle's business

My business wouldn't exist but for the wonderful, wide world of the Web. My brand exists because of the Internet. ExtraordinaryMommy began as an online reminder to moms of the "extraordinary" they were living daily. From that small platform, I introduced myself to an audience, proved my work ethic and quality product, forged relationships with others, and have been lucky enough to build a business for myself in the online media and video realm. I have a Web site and regularly use social media engagement tools, including Twitter, Facebook, and LinkedIn, for my work. The Internet is the lifeblood that feeds everything I do. I don't think I could make it through a day without communicating via Skype, asking for help via Twitter, or posting a video to YouTube. I get a little twitchy at the thought of being disconnected, so I travel with my laptop, my iPhone, and a Clear wifi card.

Aliza's business

My current business is a mobile strategy consultancy and mobile apps production company. I work entirely from home, and because I live in a rural area, I have very little face time with clients or potential clients. To get my business off the ground, I built a Web site to outline what I offered; teamed up with several apps programmers and an illustrator; and began promoting what I do to my contacts, friends, and family. All the work I do takes place on my laptop and on the Web, including writing mobile marketing plans; mapping out app specifications; receiving and reviewing illustrations from my illustrator; delivering app elements to my programmers; and presenting app screenshots and videos to clients.

Freelance Is a Business

While we're clearly recommending that you start small, we don't want you to think small. Think of yourself as an independent businessperson and not a "freelancer." Yes, labels can matter. You need to make a commitment to think and act like a sole proprietor. Even if you say you are an "independent contractor," that is a much strongor, bolder way of expressing what you do and what you're building than "I'm just freelancing." As our friend, business consultant Leah Jones, says, "Not freelancer. MORElancer. Less Free, More Lance!" You're not giving anything away for free, now, are you? We suggest that you refer to yourself as a "business owner" instead of freelancer. Now, doesn't that sound powerful?

Before we talk about some very specific Web-based businesses you can start, let's recap the types of businesses you could start. Earlier, we talked about three main types:

1) A Lifestyle Business
2) An Income Business
3) A Growing Business

Well, we did also mention a fourth: Go Big or Go Home, but this one requires some serious investment of time, money, effort, blood, sweat, tears, and teamwork to get off the ground. We'd never discourage you from that kind of major venture; however, we're here to talk about what's manageable for your specific situation (home with a baby or small children, pregnant, or planning to start a family in the near future).

"I started my consultancy because international business was my passion, but also because I saw it as an opportunity to be home with my kids — I just didn't have any kids yet," jokes Cheryl Lockhart of International Strategies, LTD, who didn't get married until a year after she launched her business, and had her first child two years later. Talk about planning for growth!

Low-Cost Internet Businesses

Let's start with some businesses that can be done using your computer and at least partially leveraging the Internet. Keep in mind that any business you start should tap into your skills, interests, and strengths — if you feel there is a major learning curve required to get started, you may want to go for something else. Stick with what you know or a variation of what you've done before. Then branch out into new areas that might call for more research or training.

We'll give you a snapshot of the following businesses:

- Internet Marketing
- Professional Blogging
- Social Media Marketing
- Virtual Assistance
- Marketing Communications
- An Online Store

These aren't the only types of online businesses you can start, of course, but they are established and reputable ways of bringing in income while basing your business from home. Each requires a different set of skills and varying costs for setup, but they all start with you having the right skills plus a good computer and Internet connection.

The online businesses outlined in this chapter have pretty basic start-up costs. The priciest items will probably be:

$1,000 for a computer
+
$500 for a 4-in-1 machine that is a printer, fax, scanner, and copier. (Prices vary, but we found a bunch on Amazon.com for $500, and many for even less.)
+
$600 — estimated annual Internet access fees
_____

$2,100 Total Basic Start-up Costs for Running an Online Business

If you already have a computer and Internet connection, you're well on your way to being equipped for an online business. An "all-in-one" device is an affordable and compact way to add functionality to your office setup.

Some people may tell you not to buy an "all-in-one" machine because "what if one feature breaks?" The price for a multifeature device can run as low as $100, so if you don't have a product warranty or it runs out, you can probably afford a replacement. If your work requires heavy usage of one part of a multifeature device, then separate that out and buy it. For example, if a scanner is critical to your work, buy a 3-in-1 device (printer, fax, copier), then purchase a higher-quality scanner. Most Internet-based businesses won't put a huge amount of wear and tear on a multifeature device solution.

No matter what business you start from home, you may also need to spend money on some or all of the following:

1. Professional services (bookkeeper, accountant, lawyer).
2. Filing fees for setting up your business name or business entity.
3. Business licensing fees.
4. Marketing tools, such as a Web site, business cards, and online ads.
5. Business and professional organization memberships, such as trade associations, your local chamber of commerce, and women's business networking groups.
6. General office supplies. You may find that with an Internet business, you tend to use fewer supplies, so you may want to refrain from buying anything until you see a specific need. For example, the chance of you using a stapler or Scotch tape dispenser as an Internet marketer is pretty slim. They are nice to have around but aren't essentials.

In Chapter 3, we'll walk you through the steps of fleshing out your business plan and setting up the legal side of your business structure. For now, we're just brainstorming, so let's look more closely at these businesses so you know what you might be getting into, including some ballpark figures for costs that you can anticipate. Also see Chapter 7 for specific ideas for promoting your company, some of which will involve additional costs.

Internet Marketing

An Internet marketing business requires very little money to get started, except for a computer and Internet connection, but you need specific skills to succeed. A strong background in marketing plus an understanding of Internet-specific marketing techniques are important. Often, women who start marketing businesses from home have held marketing jobs or had marketing duties at their previous jobs before branching out on their own.

What the business entails:
In its simplest form, Internet marketing means promoting something online; however, Internet marketing is more complex and varied. These days, Internet marketing could include e-mail marketing, Web advertising and marketing, Web development, and maybe even search engine marketing and Search Engine Optimization (SEO), which is a more specialized online marketing skill that promotes Web sites by obtaining higher rankings on search engines. We list social media

marketing separately because it is a newer area of online marketing, but it is a perfect example of how Internet marketing continues to grow and evolve over time, based on new technological developments online.

Skills and interests you should have:

According to Lori Gama, owner of DaGama Web Studio, an Internet marketer needs a wide range of Internet skills, including keyword research and analysis, e-mail marketing, and search engine marketing. You should also have:

- An understanding of the differences between online and offline marketing.
- Familiarity with various online platforms where advertising and marketing take place and how each operates (e-mail newsletter software, search engines, ad networks, blog publishing platforms, etc.).
- Strong written communications skills.
- Specialized skills, such as SEO, or a niche focus, such as podcast or blog marketing.

If you don't know anything about marketing or lack Internet marketing skills, this may not be the business for you. Be realistic about your skill level.

In addition to basic start-up costs, you may also benefit from membership in a relevant trade association, such as the International Internet Marketing Association (IIMA), for $199 per year, or the American Marketing Association (AMA), for $195 per year. To stay on top of your game, you might invest time and money in attending an industry conference or workshop. Those costs can range from hundreds to thousands (on the higher end if travel is involved). Web 2.0 Expo and Blogworld Expo are two relevant national conferences with strong online marketing tracks.

"Way back in 1996, I fell in love with the Internet after buying our first computer," says Lori. "I saw the Internet as my 'way out' of my humdrum 9-to-5 job and a way to help people while making money and staying home to raise my son." By 2000, Lori's Internet marketing business was a full-time endeavor. Lori has the benefit of being an early adopter of the Internet, which gave her an advantage to starting an Internet marketing business sooner than most people.

Like a lot of Internet marketers, Lori offers an array of services in addition to Internet Marketing and SEO. She is also a Web developer, offers branding consulting, and more recently added social media marketing to her services list. Having diverse service offerings can be a good way to grow your business and attract more clients.

Professional Blogging

If you have a gift with words and writing is one of your most favorite things to do, you may want to start a business where you write for a living. A great Web-based writing business is offering professional blogging services. As a professional blogger, you provide blog content for a variety of clients, from blog publications that hire independent bloggers, to other small businesses or organizations that don't have the resources to do their own blogging, or even major corporations looking to hire out blogging duties.

What the business entails:

Composing blog posts. Sometimes requires research, interviewing people, and sourcing photographs and illustrations to include with the posts. Could include sending content as a text file or Word document or submitting it through a content management system. May also include setting up, following, or managing an editorial calendar.

Skills and Interests you should have:

- Excellent writing skills.
- Strong understanding of the differences between online and offline writing.
- Knowledge of Basic HTML and a variety of blog publishing platforms and content management systems.
- Familiarity with stock photo usage and how to obtain them to illustrate posts (not necessary for all blogging work, but helpful).
- Ability to set up or work by an editorial calendar and adhere to deadlines.

If your grammar, spelling, and punctuation skills leave something to be desired, professional blogging — or writing, for that matter — may not be a good business option. Also, if you can't write under pressure or are terrible with deadlines, you may not do well with the often rapid or frequent nature of blogging.

Kris Bordessa blogs for several specialized sites, providing content on a near-weekly basis. She also blogs on her own site, Attainable Sustainable — not as a way to make money, but to build interest for a book project she's working on. Her specific writing services include blogging, copywriting, and even a little bit of public relations. Her clients range from large Web-based businesses, for whom she blogs about parenting and travel, to traditional brick-and-mortar businesses. She has even written content for realtors, wineries, and Grammy Award–winning musicians.

"I didn't necessarily start a blogging business," Kris admits. "I started a writing business that evolved to include blogging as technology changed." Her main start-up costs? A computer and an Internet connection.

Hadassah Sabo Milner ghostwrites posts for blogs other than her own, and also offers proofreading and editing services as well as content "curation," which means gathering and organizing content from other sources. Her main client is an online food site, JoyofKosher, and she works as content manager for their recipes and blog posts, and even manages the blog's social media.

"I started blogging for fun three years ago," recounts Hadassah. "I needed a place to just air my thoughts and feelings and found that I was good at it."

Carving out a niche for herself and gaining exposure for her online presence led her to her career and business as a professional blogger.

What about additional costs beyond the basics for starting up? A lot of professional bloggers purchase the *AP Stylebook*, either spiral-bound for $18.95 or an online subscription for $25.00 per year, or they might get *The Chicago Manual of Style* for $65.00 or $35.00 per year. Sometimes your clients might request one writing style reference book over the other or not require them at all. You'll want to purchase the same software that your clients are using if they request content delivered to them as an attached document, and most people use Microsoft Word 2010 ($139.99). You might be better off buying Microsoft Office Home and Student 2010 for $149.99, because it also includes Excel, PowerPoint, OneNote, and Outlook. (Mac users can get the 2008 version.) Office Professional 2010 includes the same applications plus Access and Publisher for $499.99. If your blogging responsibilities also require working with photos or images, you may want to purchase Photoshop Elements for about $140 to do light photo editing, or you can use a free online photo-editing service such as Picnik.com.

Since you are dealing with electronic content and documents, you should also look into an off-site backup system that automatically backs up regularly. Carbonite ($59 per year) and Mozy (starting at $5.99 per month) are two popular online backup options.

If you find that being a member of a professional or trade association is beneficial, you can join The American Society of Journalists and Authors if you can provide published news clips (or list published books). The cost is a $75 initiation fee, $50 application fee, and $195 per year for membership. Most writing associations include bloggers these days. Check out organizations such as the National Federation of Press Women at $74 per year for national membership, plus a fee to join their affiliated state chapter. There are also state-specific writers' organizations and groups where bloggers can gain support from peers and insights into making a living as a writer.

While there are bloggers out there who make money off their own blogs, we aren't recommending that as a start-up business, because it can take a very long time to build up significant traffic to your blog to then "sell" to advertisers. If you're looking to make money off your own blog, you're really more in the publishing and advertising business rather than simply being paid to write.

One woman who has built a successful business from her blog is Ponn Sabra of AmericanMuslimMom.com. Ponn methodically planned her blog as a business from the get-go and focused a lot of time and energy in coming up with revenue-generating opportunities that would become more and more viable as her Web traffic increased.

"I did my keyword research, I mapped out high-quality SEO tactics, I researched my target market — their needs and desires — and chose my URL strategically," Ponn explains. "My intentions were to make my blog a profitable online business."

Ponn has built traffic to her site by tapping into her PR skills. She has also received coverage in the media and was part of a social media campaign to help promote a CNN documentary about Muslims in America. The CNN project increased her traffic tenfold in a single day, causing the Web server hosting her blog to crash. Other than technical difficulties, the increase in traffic has only bolstered her ability to earn money from her blog.

How does Ponn make money from her blog? Her biggest revenue generator is affiliate marketing. Affiliate marketing is a relationship between a business with goods or services for sale and "affiliates" who will promote and sell these items on their Web sites or blogs for a commission, usually a small percentage of each sale. For example, the major bookseller Amazon has an affiliate program, and anyone can feature and "sell" books on their Web sites or blogs. Book sales are actually processed through Amazon, and the affiliates get a commission on each sale. Ponn also sells sponsorship and advertising on her blog, including text links and buttons.

"I've been blessed to get little donations with prayers of thanks to me and my family," Ponn adds. There is a Donate button on her blog's homepage, and she accepts donations via PayPal and can accept major credit cards and electronic checks as well.

Another way you could potentially make money via your own blog is through downloadable e-books on niche topics that people will pay to download so they can access the information you publish. To make enough money, however, you still need large amounts of traffic to your blog to convert visitors into customers. You also need great sales tools and marketing ability to convince people to pay you for content they might otherwise get online for free on someone else's blog. If you want to earn money for blogging, then blogging for someone else who pays you for the content you produce can be a more reliable business idea, and you can start making money as soon as you land your first client.

Social Media Marketing

With new technology developments on the Internet and with computers and mobile devices, social media marketing has really taken off. Social media consists of the tools, platforms, and sites that facilitate conversations and the publishing and sharing of information between people online. Social media marketing is the strategic use of these tools, platforms, and sites to promote products or services, or to disseminate information.

You can start a business offering social media marketing services to individuals, nonprofit organizations, and companies looking for someone to help them, navigate blogs, microblogs, and the myriad of social networks. Just having your own social network accounts doesn't mean you've got what it takes to consult others about their social media efforts. However, if you can combine a deep knowledge of social media tools with marketing and communications skills, you may be able to carve out a nice, flexible, and specialized online business for yourself.

What the business entails:

Can include reviewing existing online and social media assets and making strategic recommendations for improving or enhancing them, as well as setting up and managing social networks and other social media tools. You can advise on integrating social media tools and tactics into your clients' existing marketing efforts. You should also offer measurement and analysis to help clients determine if they are getting a good return on their investment (ROI) in social media marketing.

Skills and interests you should have:

- Passion for being online and engaging in online community.
- Excellent marketing, communications, and community-building skills.
- Understanding of social media marketing principles.
- Thorough knowledge of the top tier and secondary social media tools.

If you don't like participating in online communities, you may not enjoy running a business like this. If you aren't curious about how technology affects the way we communicate and don't love thinking strategically about online marketing in an ever-evolving landscape, this business is not ideal for you.

Lisa Kalner Williams started her social media marketing company, Sierra Tierra Marketing, with about $200 for a Web site and business cards. She already had a computer, an Internet connection, and social media skills. She started her business when her daughter was three years old and arranged for daycare within walking distance from her home office so she could work about four days a week.

As her business has grown, she has been able to buy additional computer peripherals, and to pay to attend industry conferences, including the Social Media Success Summit. She's also been able to afford to buy social media tools and applications such as HootSuite Pro. She hires contractors to help her in areas that weren't her forte, such as manipulating graphics in Photoshop and Facebook application development.

Like any consultant in a specialized and technical industry, you can spend money on a number of things, including subscriptions to useful tools and services such as PitchEngine.com for publishing social media releases ($39 per month for unlimited pitches) and HootSuite Pro to manage social network communications ($5.99 per month). Because social media marketing requires light graphics work, like professional blogging, investing in Photoshop Elements or using Picnik.com would be handy.

You may also choose to spend hundreds or thousands of dollars attending industry conferences to keep up with the latest technology. Local events will be more affordable — and easier to arrange childcare. National events, while more costly overall, might offer an on-site daycare service, particularly tech conferences geared toward women and parents like BlogHer, BlissDom, and Type-A Parent.

Don't invest a lot of money in anything until you've started making revenue or are somehow able to sign contracts with clients. I always kept ahead of my costs, and that does wonders for your feeling of accomplishment.

—Sarah Gilbert, online content developer

Virtual Assistance

According to Stephanie Lee of Scratchpad Secretaries, being a virtual assistant is much different than being an assistant in a corporate setting.

"You have to be on top of online applications, social media trends, and the latest in Internet marketing methods because you will use all of these systems to power and operate your business, as well as to help your clients' businesses run more smoothly and with more efficiency," says Stephanie, who also runs Moms Who Mean Business, an online business start-up and training program for moms who want to start viable home-based businesses.

Stephanie recommends setting up a system from the start that lays out your work schedule and your clients' work schedules. Time-tracking applications are very important in a virtual assistance business. Some virtual assistants use an online product called Harvest to track time and prepare invoices.

"We're not punching in at 9 and out at 5 but spending our days working on many different projects that are billable to many different people, and we've got to track that for invoicing, reporting to the client, tracking tasks, and quoting future projects, etc.," Stephanie explains.

What the business entails:

Can run the gamut from calendar management and scheduling and travel arrangements to file organization and light Internet research. You can choose to specialize your virtual assistance business based on a particular industry, such asworking for real estate agents or tech entrepreneurs, or by specific services such as personal social network profile management or schedule coordination. Many virtual assistance businesses take a "jack-of-all-trades" approach.

Skills and interests you should have:

- Highly organized with excellent time management.
- Computer and Internet proficiency.
- Word processing and spreadsheet skills.
- Excellent communications skills including e-mail and phone communications.
- Familiarity with a wide variety of online sites and tools.

If you hate following instructions or having projects delegated to you, then running a virtual assistance business probably won't work for you. Ditto if you struggle with having other people dependent on you or if you crack easily under pressure.

Depending on how mobile and accessible you need to be, chances are you'll need a smartphone, and those can start at $50 with a two-year mobile plan. You will also need to pay for your mobile phone service and a monthly data plan, which can start around $50 but can run a lot higher. Get unlimited texting as part of your phone plan, especially if you will be texting to communicate quickly with your clients.

Purchasing Microsoft Office Home and Student 2010 for $149.99 or Office Professional 2010 for $499.99 will help with file management and exchange, as well as performing tasks such as composing itineraries in Word and managing expenses in Excel. Most professional VAs get a membership to the International Virtual Assistant Association (IVAA) for $137 per year.

Rebecca Buscemi started her virtual assistance business, Creative Virtual Office, while on bed rest during her second pregnancy, at home with her two-year-old. The basic costs of starting her business included obtaining a business license, registering her business with the state where she lived, and joining the IVAA. At the time, she offered basic administrative virtual assistance services to nonprofits, and health care and education professionals, focusing on the areas in which she had previously worked.

Like many home-based businesses, Rebecca's morphed over time. Today, her business is called The Savvy Women's Business Solution, and she provides fewer administrative services and more services that focus on marketing and management.

Moms Know Best

Whether it's helping clients hit — or exceed — their business goals, giving them the tools and expertise to reach their goals on their own, or figuring out a way to get clients back on their feet after a stumble, the desire to give your clients a reason to smile should fuel what you do every day.

—Lisa Kalner Williams, Sierra Tierra Marketing

Marketing Communications

There are so many different types of businesses you can start from home with little more than the right skills, a computer, and an Internet connection. Nearly every business these days has been enhanced by "the cloud," which is just another way of saying the Internet. Working in "the cloud" means using Internet-based platforms and tools to store, access, share, and distribute your work. Because of Web power, a marketing communications business is now relatively inexpensive to start and run and can offer you the kind of flexibility you really want.

The nice thing about having a marketing communications business is that with some sharp writing skills and marketing know-how, you can offer a wide array of services for offline marketing but create it all on your computer and deliver it to your clients online. You can then expand your business by adding some online marketing services as well.

What this business entails:
You can offer services including copywriting for marketing materials such as brochures and newsletters. Depending on your areas of expertise, you could also offer marketing plan development, project management, graphic design, and online content development.

What skills and interests you should have:
- A background in marketing, advertising, public relations, or other related disciplines.
- A good grasp of online marketing and content development techniques.
- Excellent communications and writing skills.
- In some cases, graphic design skills.
- Project management skills can be a plus.

If you don't like to write, steer clear of marketing communications or any other business that requires strong written skills, for that matter. If promoting other people's businesses or projects doesn't excite you, this is not the business for you.

The additional specialized software and services you purchase will depend on the particular marketing services you offer. However, any marketer will benefit from owning a good suite of office software, such as the Microsoft Office products, ranging from $149.99 to $499.99. Many traditional marketers are members of professional trade organizations, such as the American Marketing Association (AMA) for $195 per year.

Stephanie Campbell started her marketing communications company before the birth of her first child. When she launched her business, companies were downsizing and many were getting rid of their marketing departments. She saw an opportunity as small to medium-size businesses outsourced their projects. Even after having her baby, she knew she had picked the right business.

Says Stephanie, "In short, I wanted to be available. I felt it is important for me to have flexibility in my life to accommodate illnesses, trips to the doctor, or swim lessons and playdates."

Stephanie initially offered copywriting services for businesses for their Web sites, newsletters, and annual reports, reaching out to businesses in her vast network, including contacts from her previous job. These days, she also offers event planning, Search Engine Optimization (SEO) copywriting, social media strategy, media relations, brand identity and development, strategic planning, and much more.

Says Stephanie, "As in any business, you need to constantly evolve. I always make sure I have the client's best interest at heart. This is what makes this type of business interesting — every day is different, every day is a challenge, and you need to evolve and grow to survive."

In addition to being a marketer and mom with a home-based business, Stephanie is a woman who had her baby after she got her business off the ground. How did she prepare for the arrival of her baby?

Says Stephanie, "I sat down with my two main clients well before having my baby and discussed how much I could handle in the beginning and what they could expect from me. I wanted to make sure we were all on the same page."

What else did she do? She got rid of some "needy" clients, then took three months off for maternity leave and had another writer and PR person on hand to fill in as needed.

"Once I was back to work on reduced hours, I made sure to be very organized and took advantage of every moment I had," she says.

Stephanie napped with her baby in the morning, but in the afternoon she worked while her daughter slept, and then handed the little one over to her husband when he got home from his job. She squeezed in a little more work after her daughter's bedtime. On the days when she needed to catch up, her mother came over to help.

"Nothing ever goes as planned," says Stephanie. "Just know if you have a major deadline, your child will be up all night. Be sure to know your limitations, give yourself ample opportunity to finish projects knowing that you don't have the same pre-baby freedom you used to, and do the best job you can."

Moms Know Best

Read about successful businesswomen. Attend at least one conference per year where there are successful businesswomen. Find your tribe and be with them as much as you can. Your tribe can save your life. And you can do the same for them, too.

—Lori Gama, DaGama Web Studio

Selling Items Online

So you've always dreamed of having your own store, but having a "bricks-and-mortar" retail establishment is too daunting of a proposition, especially with a baby on the way or at home. Or maybe you make things or have a knack for picking things that other people like, and you just need a platform to offer these products for sale. If you're less of a service-oriented person and more into products, there are ways to sell items online through more than just eBay. We spoke with a number of women who opened up online stores in a variety of ways. Here's what we heard.

Opening an Online Store

The most important part of opening an online store is having a quality product that you can sell. The second most important thing? A well-designed Web site where you can sell your wares, but there are also behind-the-scenes elements you have to consider, including getting product to customers. Storing inventory, packaging, and shipping your products are all part of a process known as "fulfillment," and without these critical steps, you won't have happy customers.

What the business entails:

Creating and selling products online. You can produce items yourself or outsource to a manufacturer. The same is true regarding fulfillment of the products you produce. You also need to understand how to market and sell, as well as the mechanics of getting your products displayed online on a site where people can easily purchase them.

What skills and interests you should have:

- The ability to make something or invent something and have it produced.
- Good market research skills or the ability to hire someone to do the proper research to test the viability of your product.
- Excellent sales and customer service skills.
- Strong marketing skills.

If don't have the ideas, inspiration, or wherewithal to produce products or source products, (which means selecting other people's products to sell), you probably don't want to be in the business of selling products. If you're not customer-service oriented, a products business may not be for you because it will be very customer focused.

As we've mentioned previously, a products business will have more start-up costs than a service business and more complexity in terms of preparation and steps to setting it up. But that doesn't mean it can't be done! Here are some possible expenses you'll face when launching a products company.

Estimated initial expenses:

$1,000 — computer
+ $500 — 4-in-1 machine (i.e., printer, fax, scanner, copier)
+ $1,800 — estimated annual Internet access fees (higher bandwidth at $150/month)
+ $1,000 — attorney's fees for patents and trademarks
+ $755 — patent and trademark filing fees (for one product)*
+ $75 — ecommerce software setup fees**

$+$ $2,000 — initial Web site design
$500 — camera for product photography

$7,630 Total Estimated Start-up Costs Related to Selling Products Online (this is a very rough estimate)

*Not every product can be patented, but if you come up with an original name for something you've created, you should trademark that name.

**Note that most ecommerce sites have up-front costs and then will take a small percentage of each transaction as well, so keep this in mind as you estimate costs of doing business. Every site's fees vary.

What other costs might you face with a products company? Before you even begin making too much product, you should do market research to make sure there is a market for your product. Market research can be expensive, although you can do some of it on your own through Internet research and tapping into your own network (if you know people who represent your ideal customer). You may also have to pay to produce a prototype of your product. If it is something handmade that only you can make, you'll want to get feedback on the item or items you are producing, to check for everything from quality to appeal to safety issues, such as a choking hazard.

If you're having products made by a third party, there may be manufacturing fees. These can vary, and you'll need to price your products above the costs of getting them produced in order to make a profit. Many home-based products businesses start out doing in-house fulfillment, meaning storing their own inventory, packaging, and shipping products. As they grow, they might turn to a fulfillment house when they can't do it on their own anymore and pay fulfillment fees. These vary as well.

Michelle Cloney is a single mom to 18-month-old Lucie and the inventor of Le bibble baby bottle bib, which she invented when her baby was three months old.

"We were having very messy bottle feedings, and I decided there had to be a way to prevent bottles from leaking. I designed a cloth collar using fun designer fabrics, each with an organic cotton underlay to wipe dribbles," says Michelle.

The Le bibble attaches to the baby bottle to capture the leaks before hitting baby's skin. Michelle made over a hundred prototypes before deciding on the final design. Then she found a local sewing subcontractor/manufacturer via the Internet to make the Le bibble for her, beginning with a batch of 1,500 in ten fabric choices. Michelle began selling the product online on her own Web site soon after.

Michelle says she has invested about $8,000 into her business, paying for the production labor costs, the fabrics and materials, her Web site design, a patent attorney who also did her trademark, a decent Single Lens Reflex (SLR) camera to take high-quality product photographs for her site, monthly Internet fees, product packaging, the labels that she designed herself, and the shipping materials. Whew! Since she was only selling one product, Michelle decided to go with her own online store. To find shopping cart software, she Googled "shopping software," and after reading several reviews, she went with Big Commerce, based on its positive ratings and because it was very user friendly.

As soon as someone places an order on her site, the ecommerce software on her Web site contacts her via e-mail. She packages the product, gets the shipment ready, and then literally presses "shipped" — an admin feature in the software — to let the buyer know the package has shipped. She also uses Shipworks mailing software to download all of her orders onto labels that she can print and affix to packages. Aside from packaging, it takes her five minutes from getting the order notification to shipping each order.

One thing Michelle found necessary with selling product online was organizing her inventory space since she's doing the fulfillment herself.

"I think you need to make sure you have room to hold the inventory and a system for packaging/preparing orders/shipping since you're doing it from home," she explains. "I live in a one bedroom and found it important to be organized so that the space works efficiently, since I'm at home and use the space for living and for my daughter to play."

Michelle was kind enough to provide us with her list of additional starting costs to share with you. These would be on top of the estimated initial expenses we outlined previously. Michelle and many start-up products companies take care of inventory storage and fulfillment to avoid paying fulfillment fees.

- $15/mo — Shipworks mailing software
- $16/mo — Endicia postage software, plus cost of postage (cover this in "shipping and handling" fees)
- $25/mo — Big Commerce ecommerce system
- $19/mo, plus 2–3% of each sale — Merchant Account to accept credit cards
- $142 — HTTPS Secure Server Certification (for secure online transactions)

As you can see, setting up a secure online store involves a lot of moving parts, setup costs, and monthly fees if you do it entirely from scratch.

Another products business owner is Kimberley Mulla of Kimberley's Kitchen, who sells handcrafted gourmet marshmallows and confections. Kimberley made an initial investment of about $200 in supplies, equipment, and marketing materials and says she made it back in her first hour of sales at her first market. Since then, all of her profits have been reinvested in equipment, supplies, testing new recipes, and marketing.

"Because I make an artisan product, my ingredients are expensive," Kimberley explains. "I use organic vanilla beans and fair trade, organic cocoa. I produce everything fresh to order and in small batches. I care about using quality ingredients and responsible packaging, so I invest a fair amount in my product."

Some of Kimberley's other start-up costs included marketing, her Web site domain, printed materials, and professional photography. She kept her online store setup costs very low by creating a site on Blogger.com because, she admits, it was free and simple. She uses Paypal integrated into her site to take payments for retail sales, although she gets a fair amount of custom and wholesale orders that keep her busy. On occasion, she says she has to "close" her site to stop taking orders so she can catch up.

Her advice to other moms wanting to sell something online?

"Start simple. Start with only a few items, even if you have ideas to do more. Also, sell what you want to be famous for. If you want to be famous for one thing, don't put a lot of energy into something else."

Selling Through Etsy

While there are many sites you can use to set up an online store, a very popular marketplace and community for crafters and other product creators is Etsy. From jewelry, to accessories, to party favors, you name it, women — especially moms working from home — have set up shop to sell their creative wares.

Nikki Hart of Sweethearts Shoppe, an accessories store, originally chose a site called Zibbet to sell her products online. She was attracted to the fact that it was new and didn't charge listing fees, so it was a great way to keep her costs down.

"After promoting constantly online, there just wasn't enough traffic targeting on Zibbet, so I had to rethink what I was doing," Nikki explains. "I knew Etsy was a very well-known place for women. Sure they had listing fees and selling fees, but if you think of the costs to promote and to get your brand out there, you have to do what's right for your company."

Since signing up with Etsy, Nikki's business has taken off. Her online store has received good traffic, she's getting a lot of positive feedback from potential customers, and her sales are growing.

Jodie Valenti is a party designer/stylist and a cake designer. She has two companies. Yes, you heard us right. Her companies are complementary: Party NV as well as Cakes, Cupcakes

& Cookies . . . OH MY! She also has two young boys under five and an 11-year-old stepson she and her husband have every other week. Oh my is right!

Jodie has an Etsy store for her party design business. She creates party decorations and favors mostly on her computer using Adobe Creative Suite, a design software suite. She also uses various scrapbooking and crafting tools like a glue gun to assemble her products.

For Party NV, she couldn't decide between setting up an online store on Etsy or on eBay.

"In the end I decided on Etsy. I feel that it is a much nicer setup, plus it's gaining in popularity," explains Jodie. She felt people were getting "burned out" on eBay.

Setting up her Etsy store was a cinch for Jodie. She just went onto the site, set up her store profile, and started listing items. The biggest challenge she says she faced was trying to organize herself once orders started coming in and her products started selling.

Of course, she does her share of marketing and has a Facebook Page for both of her businesses, as well as a blog for Party NV, where she showcases her custom party decorations in blog posts with photos.

> *Be honest about your value, too . . . don't sell super cheap in the hopes to make sales. You'll end up working for nothing and that won't be any fun. Make sure you figure out your material and packaging costs and then add in your time . . . this is how you should be pricing!*
>
> —Jodie Valenti, Party NV and Cakes, Cupcakes & Cookies . . . OH MY!

If you have the skills, there are many businesses that you can start that are powered by a computer and the Internet. The service-oriented businesses tend to be less costly to start up. Selling products will most likely require more initial outlays of cash. Regardless, you should choose the business you'll start from home based on what you know, what you can do, and what you'll love to do. We encourage you to keep things manageable to set yourself up for nothing but success!

Chapter 3
Building Blocks for Your New Business

When starting a business, there always seems to be so much to do. Where do you start? First, come up with a name for your business, then put together a written plan, assemble a Business A-Team who can help you cross every "t" and dot every "i," and make sure you comply with any local, state, or national requirements for running a business. Sounds simple, right? But, in fact, you need to apply care, thought, and perseverance every step of the way. We'll walk you through the process so you can benefit from our experience and the wisdom of a number of other moms who've successfully launched their own start-up businesses.

Naming Your Business

Let's begin with naming your business. You'll want to create a name that reflects what your business is about or communicates clearly how your product or service can benefit the consumer. Keep in mind, as you begin to develop your new company, that the name might change to better reflect what you're planning to offer. Also, you may find that, after you speak to a lawyer, your business name may have to change again if your favorite moniker is already in use by someone else and there might be a trademark conflict.

Naming your business could be as simple as using your own name: Jane Doe Consulting, Debbie Jones and Associates, or Sue Smith Internet Marketing. Coming up with a business name can seem daunting because you need to consider several things:

1. A name that at least somewhat conveys who you are or what you do.
2. A name that is easy to remember and hopefully easy to spell.
3. A name that doesn't infringe on someone else's trademark.

Oh-oh, the last one sounds a little scary. Have no fear. Later in this chapter, we'll talk about building your Business A–Team, including a lawyer who can help you navigate things like trademark searches and applications.

Here are some business names, along with each company's tagline and what the company does. One thing to note is that when you come up with a name for your company — which can also be referred to as your "brand" — less obvious names require more marketing muscle to help people understand who you are and what you do. A good tagline can help.

Company Name	Tagline	What They Do
Mediaegg	Mobile with purpose, Meaningful apps	Mobile marketing consulting and mobile apps production
DanielleSmithMedia.com	At the intersection of social and media	Correspondent, spokesperson and speaker, media trainer
Katie Newman Gifts and Home	Treasures that will tickle you pink	Online boutique of gifts and home accents
Cutie Pa Tutus, LLC	A whole new "spin" on tutus	Children's apparel and play clothing
Aqua Tails, LLC	Where's your tail?	Mermaid swim tails (costumes)
Frittabello, LLC	Inspired gifts for a baby's life journey	Baby gifts
Maternal Instinct	Creative problem solvers for marketing to moms	Ad agency that specializes in the mom market

Once you think you have the name — and even the tagline — that you'd like to use for your business, come up with one or two alternatives just in case you can't use your first choice.

Every business owner will probably have a specific story about why they chose the business name they are using. Laura White-Ritchie came up with her company name — BrainyFeet — as a reference to something she read in the Dr. Seuss book *Oh, the Places You'll Go!* that motivated her to leave her day job and go out on her own.

"The entire book is relevant to anyone who's making a life-altering change such as starting a business, because you want your family to be the nexus of your life," Laura says of the Dr. Seuss favorite. But deciding to go with such a whimsical and abstract name wasn't a quick decision for Laura.

"I spent almost seven years nurturing a reputation as an authority on microenterprise development," she explains. As she started her online-based business, Laura says she knew her name wasn't going to be an immediate draw.

"I was still nervous that by creating a separate business name, I would be limiting my ability to be well-known for my expertise," says Laura, but now she feels connected to her company name. "It's been great! We're a society raised on Seuss, so most people just 'get it' and know instantly what I'm all about."

Amanda Moreno Duke of Cutie Pa Tutus explained that she called both her children "cutie pa tootie" from time to time, and her company name was a spin on that phrase.

"It also embodied what we do," says the maker of tutus, costumes, and other fun clothing for kids. "We wanted a certain amount of intuitiveness about our name, both for the ease of securing a Web domain and for search engine purposes. It was an added bonus that we thought the name was cute!"

As a business owner, Amanda highly recommends thoroughly researching your company name to be certain that someone else isn't using it already.

"Not only do you not want to be inadvertently competing on search engines for your target market, but you also don't want to be violating trademark law and then incurring a lot of unnecessary expenses for your company when you have to change its name," she says.

Once you've figured out a name for your company, you should also check on the Web to see if you can get the domain name for your new company, so your Web site is branded as well.

"If only I knew then how important domain names are and how much more effective they are when your key word is in them, I would have made things easier on myself," says Scarlet Paolicchi of Moms Wear Your Tees Social Media Marketing.

Scarlet's business is social media marketing. Her important key words are "social media marketing." But her domain name is MomsWearYourTees.com.

"I had no idea at the time that the domain served as anything more than a name," she says. "Now it seems like common sense that it would alert search engines to your site purpose."

Scarlet has been working on solutions to her domain name dilemma, including rebranding her blog. She is considering getting a new domain, which would also entail making Web site graphic changes, all of which are unanticipated expenses.

See Chapter 7 for more details on obtaining and using your domain name.

Business Plan Basics

Planning is a very important step toward making your business idea a reality and putting you on a path toward a successful business. Still, many of us tend to fly by the seat of our pants when it comes to starting and running a business. Trust us when we say that planning is really important and beneficial in the long run.

"I wish I would have listened to the experts who said having a business plan was key to having a business," says Jennifer Covello, founder of Frittabello, LLC, a baby gifts company. "Since I had over 25 years of corporate experience in product and brand management, PR, marketing, etc., I thought I could do this 'all in my head.' I now see how critical it is to have a plan with solid financials, in order to have a thriving business as opposed to a nice hobby."

Jennifer did eventually put together a first draft of her business plan and says it helped her focus on the real mission of her business.

"I think not having a plan impacted me most financially. I did not have a firm grasp on the numbers," Jennifer admits. "My business plan helped me see that I really needed to tie my marketing and sales activities to clear revenue goals."

We've turned to our friend Carol Roth, entrepreneur and business consultant, to guide us as we think about business plans.

"If you fail to prepare, you prepare to fail. Boy Scouts know to be prepared. I don't know anyone who ever said 'I wish I had been less prepared for that — it was really a waste of my time to prepare,'" says Carol.

By writing a business plan, you not only prepare for running your company, but you can work out the kinks and any potential problems and issues before they happen. But don't worry: business plans don't have to be long and are not written in stone. They are more like road maps to guide you in the right direction to help you run your business well.

While business plans can vary in length and format, there are some sections that are considered standard and that any professional or potential investor reviewing your plan will expect to see.

Here are the elements that Carol recommends we all think about as we begin writing our business plan:

1. WHAT DOES YOUR COMPANY DO?

Carol suggests that when you are stating what you do, you should be able to do it in one or two concise sentences. Make sure that potential clients or customers can readily understand the value of what you do from your "elevator pitch" description. Your one to two sentences about your company should answer the customer's question, "What's in it for me?" Put yourself in the customer's shoes for this part.

What does that mean exactly? Well, you could say, "I make cute purses because I like cute purses," but this leaves your customer out of it, says Carol.

A better company description might be, "I make purses that keep busy, working moms organized for anything that happens in their day." All about the customer!

To be successful and to be taken seriously in business, take the focus off yourself, and be very aware of your customers. How does your business benefit them? If they don't buy your product and services, you do not have a business, right?

Have a fantastic network of friends, family, and people you trust that are able to give you a few hours a week that you can spend solely on running your business. Even if it's only three hours a week, it's imperative to have time to be still and focus on your business goals.

—Robin Ernst, Thrive Advertising

Start with answering these questions:

What will your company do?

What need are you solving for your customer? Emphasize benefits!

What unique skills/aspects do you bring to the table that are different from and better than those of your competition?

When you articulate benefits to the customer, these could be financial, time-saving, spiritual, and physical. Be specific about how you solve a need that customers may have — and that you offer something unique that your competitors don't!

2. BUSINESS MODEL (Translation: How Will Your Company Make Money?)

How do you plan on making money here? What is your process for making money? Sometimes, we can get so focused on the idea for our business that we neglect to figure out this essential aspect of any business: how we're going to get paid.

Not sure if your business idea is viable? Why not do informational interviews with other businesspeople with businesses similar to the one you want to start and ask them how they generate revenues?

For example, say that you want to make money from your blog. Ask other bloggers about their business model, such as how much traffic they get and how much they charge for advertising (this shouldn't be secret information). If you are getting 500 visitors per month and they are getting 50,000, clearly they can turn that traffic into revenue — but can you realistically do the same with a fraction of the traffic? Most bloggers who have turned their blogs into businesses will often provide advertising information, including statistics about their audience size or site traffic. Many bloggers are very willing to share information with others who are hoping to start a blog business. Still others teach about turning a blog into a business (see Problogger, Thursday Bram, and The Sits Girls and their Bloggy Boot Camp conferences).

How will your business make money? (This can also be referred to as your "business model" or your "revenue streams.")

3. THE MARKET and COMPETITION

Writing about the market for your services or products — as in your "target market" — as well as identifying your competition is part of any traditional business plan. The idea behind these questions is to help you identify your business opportunities and examine who is in a similar space with a business like yours or in the same industry space as yours. This is a good way to think about the lay of the land ahead of you as you begin to build and grow your own company.

You can download this worksheet at MomIncorporated.com.

Who is your target market? Be very specific. The answer is not "Everyone."

Are they male, female, or both?

How old are they, approximately?
Or what "demographic" do they fit into? Boomers, Moms, Teens, or Tweens? If your product is for children, your actual target market is their parents, not the kids themselves.

Why would they want or need your product or service?

Who else offers products or services similar to yours?

Don't say "Nobody," because even if you think you've invented the most unique thing in the world, there is always someone else out there who is competing for your customers.

What are your competitors doing really well?

Maybe they have a great product name or their Web site rocks. Be objective and specific.

What are your competitors doing poorly?

Are they terrible on Twitter? Do they fail to explain who they are and what they do? Are there a lot of unanswered complaints about them online?

What can you do BETTER than your competition?

These should be things you can actually do, not vague things like "Be great."

4. MARKETING

How are you going to get clients or customers? Come up with at least seven specific tactics to market your company. How are you going to cut through the noise and reach people? We'll go into more detail about marketing and promotion in Chapter 7.

Smart Ways to Market Your Company

1. **Spread the Word:** Send an e-mail to your entire list of contacts, letting them know about your new business and offer a referral discount.
2. **Be Social:** Create a presence in popular social networks for your new company and invite your personal and professional contacts to connect with you there.
3. **Go to Print:** Develop printed collateral such as business cards, postcards, and fliers to promote your company.
4. **Network, Network, Network:** Attend business networking events to distribute marketing materials and talk about your business with prospective customers who could also refer customers to you.
5. **Get Listed:** List your company in business directories, including Web-based ones.
6. **Get Published:** Submit prewritten articles or blog posts with great tips and information based on your expertise. Try a trade or chamber newsletter or a blog that reaches your target market, or even your local newspaper.
7. **YouTube It!** Create a fun, short video to demo your product or promote your services and upload it to YouTube. You can capture screenshots and your voice, easily making a screencast on Screenr.com or add audio to a slideshow on Slideshare.net or even use cute cartoon characters to "read" your script at Xtranormal.com.

Include the tactics that you'll want to utilize to market your business below or download this worksheet from MomIncorporated.com. Be creative!

Marketing Tactic 1:
Marketing Tactic 2:

Marketing Tactic 3:
Marketing Tactic 4:
Marketing Tactic 5:
Marketing Tactic 6:
Marketing Tactic 7:

5. SHORT- AND LONG-TERM GOALS

Now let's zoom out and look at the bigger picture. What do you want to get out of your business? A business goal is something that can be met if you run your business well and stay focused on meeting that goal. Business goals are concrete and attainable, meaning you can actually reach them. "Being the best consultant ever" isn't a business goal, although it might be an underlying personal goal (even though it isn't clear what "being the best" means). Business goals are clear, and you can attach measurable points to them, such as making a certain amount of revenue or increasing the number of clients in a certain time period by a specific percentage.

What do you want your company to look like? What is your actual END GOAL that you are trying to reach? All other parts of your plan must align with your end goal. This means that when you market your business, you have your business goals in mind. You might market your Web site to get more traffic. How much traffic are you getting? How many sales or inquiries? If you're just starting out and the numbers are zero, then you need to figure out the amount of sales you need per week or month to hit your financial goals for your company. Your business goals don't only include making X amount of money per month, but also getting X amount of Web-site traffic and X percentage of "conversions," meaning sales or inquiries that lead to sales.

So if you want to make $500 per month and are selling cute widgets for $10 each, you have to sell 50 of them a month. If you get 1,000 people to your Web site, and only 2.5 percent of your traffic buys something, you need to double your traffic to reach your financial goals. With 2,000 people coming to your site and 2.5 percent buying something, you are now selling 50 items per month at $10 a pop. Of course, these numbers will fluctuate all the time, but setting concrete business goals helps you understand how hard you will have to work to reach them. In this case, your short-term goal is selling 50 products per month. Your longer-term goals could be meeting or surpassing 600 items sold per year (50 x 12 months = 600 items). You could also have a long-term goal of increasing your sales over the course of the year to reach 1,000 items sold by year's end.

Let's look at a fictional start-up.

What is its name and purpose?:

Jane's Virtual Assistant Services for Authors will provide prompt, accurate research and organizational services to self-published authors to help them stay focused on their writing so they can make more money.

What are its short-term and long-term goals?:

- **Short-term:** Contact 50 authors in the first three months of business to let them know about your services.
- **Short-term:** Land contracts with three authors in first three months of business at $1,500 per contract.
- **Long-term:** Bring in $15,000 in Year 1. Jane will need at least ten clients per year to meet this. If this is unrealistic, she could either reduce her financial goal or increase her contract price.
- **Long-term:** Increase revenues by 20 percent in Year 2 and by another 20 percent in Year 3. This means an increase of $3,000 or two additional contracts in Year 2, and $3,600 or about 2.5 additional contracts in Year 3. At Jane's going rate, that puts her at more than 14 author clients in Year 3. Again, if unrealistic, she should raise her rates or rethink her overall goals. She's only one person, so she'll need to plan for what she can *actually* achieve alone. If she chooses to outsource some work, she now has to think about the expense of outside contractors.

Your business plan is a road map and not written in stone. In fact, since you are writing it before you even start your business (you *are*, right?), then you should revisit your plan after your first month of business to see if your assumptions were correct or if you need to adjust your numbers based on reality versus guesswork.

Now list some concrete short-term and long-term goals that will help you move your business forward and grow it over time.

Short-Term Goal 1:
Short-Term Goal 2:
Long-Term Goal 1:
Long-Term Goal 2:

6. MILESTONES

You need to establish points along the way that let you check in to make sure you are reaching your goals. Setting milestones can take the overwhelming nature out of your big goals and create steps that you can focus on to achieve and celebrate along the way.

Going back to Jane's Virtual Assistant Services for Authors, if her goal is to bring in $15,000 in Year 1, where does she begin? (The following might be some sample milestones that you can apply to your business as well.) Jane can:

- Build a Web site to explain her services.
- Send out an e-mail to all of her contacts, asking for a referral to a self-published author they know.
- Make a presentation at a writers' group in her area.
- Send out 15 proposals in her first month of business.
- Evaluate the response rate of the proposals she has sent out and rethink her approach and refine her proposals.
- Send out 15 more proposals in her second month of business, making any changes needed to be more effective.
- Land three contracts by the end of the third month of business.

Like we mentioned earlier in this chapter, if Jane wants to make $15,000 in Year 1, she'd have to calculate how much she needs to make per month to hit her annual financial goals. In the case of Jane, she should make at least $1,250 per month, so her contracts must add up to at least that amount, if not more. Say she offers a monthly package for self-published authors of $325 per month to provide a set number of services. She should then encourage her author clients to sign a contract with her for a year. She'd need four author clients who sign on the dotted line for a year of services (at $3,900 apiece) to reach her annual revenue goals. There are many ways to get to a financial goal.

Since nothing in business happens like clockwork, and chances are Jane may end up signing clients on a month-to-month basis or for a few months at a time, her milestones — like her plan — need to be flexible and adaptable. Jane may go months without signing a new client, and then in a single month she might sign four authors but only one for a year-long contract. As you can see, there are a lot of variables to running and growing your business and working toward your goals, so milestones help you break things down into bite-size chunks that you can manage and achieve over time. Reexamining your milestones regularly — such as every month or every quarter — is a good idea as well, to keep your plan fresh and realistic.

Milestone/Date to Achieve or Reexamine:

Milestone/Date to Achieve or Reexamine:

Milestone/Date to Achieve or Reexamine:

Milestone/Date to Achieve or Reexamine:

By setting milestones and nailing down some dates for when you hope to achieve them, you'll have a better way to track your progress and, over time, you'll better understand what milestones and timelines are realistic. Even more important, you'll see if your business goals are achievable.

Build Your Business A-Team

A typical business plan usually includes a section entitled "Team," but this is necessary only if you are planning on starting your business with others, and especially if you are thinking about seeking funding from investors. Most investors will tell you that when they invest in a company, they often look at both the business idea and the team members. Even if the business idea is a great one, without a strong team to execute it, all you really have is an idea.

Unless you are planning for a high-growth business, your business plan document is more for your own reference or to be shared with your trusted Business A-Team, such as your accountant, bookkeeper, and lawyer.

So let's talk more about your Business A-Team. You may be working from home, but you can't do it all alone — or at least you shouldn't.

My #1 piece of advice is to ask for help. Chances are, if a woman is running a business AND raising a family, she's a bit of an overachiever and *help* is often a four-letter word. Stop being silly. Ask for help.

—Stacey Vulakh, Timestyle Coaching and Consulting

Your Bookkeeper

Let's start with a bookkeeper. Your bookkeeper should take care of all your accounting and financial records for your company throughout the year, so the higher-paid CPA (Certified Public Accountant) who you hire to do your taxes doesn't have to go through your shoebox. It might be cheaper for you in the end, so you don't end up paying a CPA to do the busy work. A CPA wants to look at a balance sheet and profit-and-loss statement. Your bookkeeper can put those together for you and get them to your CPA. Who you hire is totally up to you as long as you know he or she understands your bookkeeping and accounting needs and can cover the work you need done.

Here are some questions to ask to find the right one. Thanks to bookkeeper Christie Mascelli of Assured Business Services for helping with these! You can download and print this handy checklist and use it as a guide when you're interviewing bookkeepers and accountants.

20 Questions to Ask a Bookkeeper or Accountant

About Their Business

1. What services do you offer to your clients? (Accounts payable, accounts receivable, payroll — look for all of the above.)
2. Why shouldn't I do this stuff myself? (A good answer: Stick to your specialty, your expertise, and the company and work you should be focusing on.)
3. What kinds of clients do you have? (They don't have to know your industry, but it's good if they work with similarly sized businesses. And, if your business is Web specific, you DO want someone who understands the ins and outs of tax issues for the online space.)
4. What's the best way for me to get my data to you? (It should be compatible with what you like.)
5. What steps do you take to secure my data in your possession? (Example: locked filing cabinets, safes, locked offices, security alarm system)
6. Will you handle all of my payroll, payroll taxes, and my quarterly payments? (This is all tax preparation leading into the next year, so make sure they handle this.)
7. Do you work by yourself or do you have staff? (You want to know who will be handling your finances.)
8. What hours are best for you?
9. Who will be my main contact? (If not the person you're meeting with, you probably want to meet him or her.)
10. Do you do year-end taxes? (If you are incorporating, ask: Do you do corporate returns?)
11. Do you have a CPA referral or if I have a CPA, are you comfortable working with him/her?

About Costs to You

12. What software do you use? Do I need to purchase the software myself?
13. How do you charge? Do you bill hourly or do you charge a flat monthly fee? (For hourly, you can establish a cap where you are notified when your bookkeeper exceeds a set amount of hours per month.)
14. If hourly, how many hours do you think it will take to do my bookkeeping?
15. What other kinds of charges can I expect? (Example: Payroll fees)

More About Them

16. How do you like to work? (Online, phone, in person)
17. What financial tasks do you NOT do?

18. What kind of relevant certifications, licenses, or degrees do you have? (Look for a degree in accounting or a certified bookkeeper.)

19. How many years of experience do you have bookkeeping? (Having many years of experience can count even more than degrees.)

20. Are you available for a monthly call or meeting with me to review financials? (If not, find someone who is. You need good, ongoing communication.)

Your relationship with your bookkeeper — and any consultant you hire for your business — should be based on trust and mutual respect. They will know the inner workings of your company's financial well-being, and you will be giving them access to all of your accounts. Pick someone not only qualified on paper but also someone who understands what you want from your company and how you prefer to work. Be honest with yourself about what kind of client you'll be, to avoid conflict later on.

Wendy Armbruster Bell, owner of Snugabell Mom & Baby Gear, learned the value of a good bookkeeper as she juggled her freelance business and her new online store, where she was selling a pump bra she created.

"I did my own books for my freelancing but was nine months behind on the books for Snugabell before I bit the bullet and hired a bookkeeper," Wendy admits.

While you may think you can't afford a bookkeeper, you can't afford *not* to have someone help you when it comes to finances. Don't try to wear too many hats, she advises.

Says Wendy, "When you think of the time you are freeing up by not struggling with something that is not your forte, you will more than make up for the cost of the help. Time and time again I have found this to be true."

Live by the old saying, "Think about what you would do if you knew you could not fail." If you choose to create your business from a place of passion, the natural drive you have inside will inspire and fuel you day to day.

—Natasha Stocker, Inspired Spaces Design

AT-A-GLANCE GRID: What You Can Do and What You Can/Should Outsource

Here is a breakdown of some of the most common tasks you'd want a bookkeeper or accountant to perform.

Task	Bookkeeper	Accountant
Setting up your company books	Yes	Yes
Handling accounts receivable	Yes	Yes
Handling accounts payable	Yes	Yes
Setting up payroll*	Maybe	Yes
Managing payroll*	Maybe	Yes
Estimated quarterly taxes	Yes	Yes**
End of the year taxes	Maybe	Yes**

*You can also hire a company that specializes in payroll services, but if you're a sole proprietor, this is probably unnecessary.

**You can also hire a tax accountant who focuses on tax-related support.

Keep in mind that if a bookkeeper can help you with some aspects of your company books, he or she will most likely be less expensive than an accountant doing the same thing. In fact, in many cases, your accountant may pass on some of the load to a junior accountant or bookkeeper to do the actual work. When you choose whom you want to work with, it should be based on your sense of being able to have a good working relationship with that person as much as it is on his or her skills.

Your Lawyer

Now, time to move on to a lawyer. A trusted legal adviser is like gold to any business owner. Often, people set up businesses online by themselves because they think having an attorney or accountant do it is too expensive. But paying for a one-hour consultation on business structure and operations is often helpful and affordable (many attorneys charge $200–$300 for these calls). You can then proceed with setting everything up online if you'd prefer and at least know that you have a sound business structure in place. Investing now in legal guidance could save you thousands of dollars in the future.

Having another knowledgeable person reviewing what you are doing from a legal standpoint is helpful, even if you only retain someone for a few hours of his or her time. You might even be able to get appropriate and free guidance from a counselor at your local Small Business Development Center or SCORE office as well. Let's dig into the questions you should ask a lawyer or legal adviser.

Before we go on, we want to give a big thanks to Shannon King Nash, Esq., for her extensive help with the legal and taxes portion of this chapter. Shannon is mother to three boys and author of the award-winning book, *For the Love of Money: The 411 to Taking Control of Your Taxes and Building Your Net Worth.* See, even we sought the advice of trusted experts.

12 Questions to Ask a Lawyer

What questions to ask to find the right legal adviser:

1. How much do you charge to do a basic consultation to help me to decide the best structure for my type of business/industry?
   Keep in Mind: You can always retain someone for a few hours to get expertise without breaking the bank.

2. Which is the best legal structure for my business — an LLC operating agreement, corporation bylaws and shareholder agreements, or other?
   Keep in Mind: There are pros and cons to each, but simpler may be better, at least in the beginning.

3. I plan to eventually sell my company (in a merger or acquisition). What is the best legal structure for me?
   Keep in Mind: This may sound premature, but knowing your options in case you decide to sell your business one day is helpful. You could also ask about the best structure for getting investors or for a future IPO (Initial Public Offering or "going public." Doesn't hurt to think big!)

4. Do I need business liability insurance?
   Keep in Mind: There are often industry standards for insurance, so ask around. We talk more about insurance later in this chapter.

5. What about life insurance (known as key man's insurance) to help my heirs or keep the business running if I should become incapacitated? What about disability insurance?
   Keep in Mind: As a sole proprietor, you don't have someone else on hand to run things in case something happens to you. If your business income is critical to the well-being of your family, insurance can help.

6. If I'm a sole proprietorship/DBA, do I need an employer identification number (EIN)?
   Keep in Mind: Anyone can get an EIN, especially if you anticipate having employees down the line. See more info about EINs later in this chapter.

7. How do I determine my salary from the business?

   Keep in Mind: Even though you might be putting most of the money back into the business, certain legal structures such as LLCs will treat any profits as income to you (much like a salary).

8. What are the annual business filings I have to make with the state/city for my business?

   Keep in Mind: This will vary state to state, and don't forget your city or county filings.

9. Do I need to trademark my business legal name?

   Keep in Mind: We've talked about the fact that getting a trademark is a good idea. This can be done on your own or with the help of a lawyer, or in some combination of both.

10. If I have independent contractors, what legal and tax documents do I need to make sure they complete before they start working?

    Keep in Mind: Since you're a sole proprietor, if you hire outside help, most likely it will be independent contractors.

11. Does my company have to hold an annual meeting? If so, what form should I use to prove that I did this?

    Keep in Mind: Even as a company of one, you may have some requirements for meetings and documenting the meetings, depending on your corporate structure.

12. Based on your experience, what are the most common business mistakes that business owners make — and what can I do to prevent them?

Michelle Cloney of Le bibble says she can't even imagine doing the patent filing required for the baby bottle bib she invented. Hiring a patent attorney was the first thing she did, even before finding a manufacturer. Her patent attorney performed a thorough search to see what or if there was anything else similar to her product on the market or patent pending. He explained to her how a patent was filed and the difference between a utility patent and a design patent. He even helped her to get the illustrations for her product, then filled out the patent application accurately.

"I believe if you want something important done professionally and you don't know how to do it, hire the correct person the first time," says Michelle. "It's well worth the investment — just in time saved alone!"

Naming Your Business, Legally

One of the first things you're going to want your new lawyer to check for you is whether or not the name you've come up with for your business is appropriate to use. A lawyer usually can do a trademark search for about $600–$800 or so, and then let you know if the name is in use by someone else or if you are free to claim it and use it. We also highly recommend checking to guarantee that you are not infringing on someone else's trademark *and* applying for your own trademark; however, be prepared for several hundred dollars in application fees to the Patent and Trademark Office (PTO), and then at least several more hundred dollars paid to your lawyer, in addition to the trademark search fee. When all is said and done, you may end up spending between $1,000 and $2,000 for securing your trademark, although you could also apply for your trademark on your own if you have the time, attention to detail, and patience. You can do this through the USPTO.gov Web site. The Trademark Application Electronic System (TEAS) fees are between $275 and $375 per class. A class is the classification that the PTO designates to goods and services such as "Jewelry" or "Education and Entertainment."

To trademark Cutie Pa Tutus, LLC, Amanda spent $280 and a couple of hours at her computer.

Says Amanda, "The Patent and Trademark Office has an online search for active trademarks as well as an online application, and it's not nearly as scary as it looks! I spent a lot of time doing searches to make sure that I wouldn't waste money and time filing for a name that was already taken."

She even came up with variations of the name she wanted, such as Cutie Pa Tutu, Cutiepatutus, and Cutiepa Tutuz. She did the online application for her trademark on her own. Then it took about six months before she received the official registered trademark designation in the mail.

Having her company name trademarked helped protect it on several occasions. Other Facebook Pages have appeared over time with a variation on Amanda's company name, with an "s" added or symbols in the name.

"Even though the PTO protects against slight variations, it's much more difficult to monitor a social media site like Facebook," Amanda says, explaining that when they do find pages on Facebook that infringe on her company's name, she first attempts to contact the page owner before going to Facebook to report a trademark violation. Trademark violations on some social networks can result in offending accounts being shut down.

"We know it's not going to be fun coming up with a new name and branding for their company, but we'd like to be as polite and helpful as possible about it," says Amanda. "No one wants to spend more money than they have to at the attorney's office going through with a 'cease and desist' action unless they absolutely have to."

A cease and desist action starts with a letter asking someone who is infringing on your trademark to stop using the offending name immediately, but in some cases, this can escalate to a lawsuit. Who knew there could be so much potential drama over a trademark? But when it comes down to it, a trademark is an asset of your company, whether it is your company name or a product name.

Something you should know about trademarks is that you might not be looking to secure a trademark at all, but instead, you might be getting a service mark. What is the difference? Basically, a trademark is a name, work, or image (like a logo or a cartoon character) that you will be using in trade, so a product name or a product company's name could be a trademark. If you are starting a service-oriented business — or if the mark you are using will represent services — then you protect it by getting a service mark. When Aliza had an Internet consulting company called Cybergrrl, Inc., she made sure it was registered as a service mark. Her new mobile consultancy, Mediaegg, is also a service mark. But Amanda from Cutie Pa Tutus would register her company name as a trademarks since she is selling products under that name. If she were teaching Cutie Pa Tutus workshops, she could register for a service mark to protect the use of that name for workshops and education.

One thing you might not know about registered trademarks is that you may have to wait months, if not a year, to get one. The symbol for a registered trademark is the letter R with a circle around it: ®. While you are waiting for your registration to come through, you can signify to others that you have a trademark or service mark pending by including a small "TM" or "SM" on the upper right side of your mark, i.e., your company or product name like this: Mediaegg[SM].

There are many legal ins and outs regarding trademarks and service marks. A good lawyer can make a complex process more streamlined. If you are producing original content, including text and illustrations, you should look into copyrighting your work. If you are producing a truly unique product, you may also have a lawyer look into patenting your creation. Understand that you don't have to apply for trademarks, service marks, copyrights, or patents; however, it is really a good idea to do so to protect your ownership of the things you create. We recommend it!

Structuring Your Business

Should you be an "Inc." or a "DBA"? An "LLC" or an "S corp"? All of this alphabet soup can really send your head spinning. You probably think that if you have a business, you'd better incorporate it to protect yourself from possible lawsuits or for tax reasons. But you have to ask yourself: how much legal liability do I really have, given the business I'm starting? A good lawyer and accountant can help you understand the risks and benefits of incorporating or at least creating some kind of legal structure to your company for clarity, if not for protection of some kind.

First, let's get the definitions out of the way, so we know what we're dealing with. Thanks again to Shannon King Nash, Esq., for her input here.

On with the definitions!

Sole Proprietorship. This is the simplest type of business entity that is owned and run by a single individual, and there is no legal distinction between the owner and the business — they are one and the same. All profits and all losses of this type of business are attributed to the business owner, so they are taxed as personal income on your tax return (Form 1040 Schedule C).

Doing Business As or DBA. Can also be called a Trade Name or an Assumed Business Name. This is a business name that any individual or company can use to conduct business. It is a legal business name, and you have to file with your city or state to make it legal. A person can operate a business using a DBA to have a more professional company name without setting up a separate business entity. For example, Jane Doe could be selling custom water bottle holders. Without incorporating, she could call her business H2O Holders, and open up a bank account under that name. So she is *doing business as* H2O Holders even though she is still operating as a sole proprietorship. Remember: If you are not forming a separate legal entity, you are personally responsible for any legal issues pertaining to your business.

LLC. This stands for Limited Liability Company. You can be an owner in an LLC with other people or be the only owner, called a Single Member LLC or SMLLC. An LLC is considered to be an entity or "person" separate from you, so it offers you a shield of protection if someone were to bring a business-related lawsuit against your company. Every state differs in terms of how it treats LLCs, including how much protection you'll get from running your business as one. Shannon explains that although the LLC files a tax return (Form 1065), it does not pay taxes. Instead, the owners take their share from the LLC's profits and all losses (these are shown on a Schedule K-1 form) and report this on their personal tax returns. A Single Member LLC or SMLLC is taxed like a sole proprietorship, with taxes paid by the owner of the LLC instead of the LLC business entity. The owner files only their personal taxes. The SMLLC's profits and losses are then reported directly on the owner's tax return (Form 1040 Schedule C).

Corporation. Legally, a corporate entity is also considered separate from you and is treated as a "person." Corporations issue shares, and you can be a shareholder and also a corporate employee. The legal protection comes in because the corporation is viewed separately from you, so if you've followed the guidelines for forming and maintaining a corporation, you are personally protected if the corporation is sued. The corporate entity acts as a shield to its shareholders and employees, but, like LLCs, this protection may vary from state to state and is dependent on you complying properly with the requirements of running a corporation. One such requirement in most states is that a corporation must show that shareholders are holding regular board meetings and keeping minutes.

There are two types of corporations: S corporation (also known as an S corp) and C corporation (also known as a C corp). C corporations file tax returns (Form 1120) and pay taxes on those returns. S corporations are treated like LLCs in that they file tax returns (Form 1120S) but don't pay federal income taxes. The owners report their share from the S corporation's profits and losses (shown on a Schedule K-1 form) on their personal tax returns.

Usually, S corps and C corps are designated with an "Inc." at the end of them (such as Aliza's previous company Cybergrrl, Inc. , which was an S corp). As an LLC, she can use LLC in her company name (such as Mediaegg, LLC) or choose not to use any designation and just refer to the company as Mediaegg.

Both an S corp and a C corp are separate legal entities created by filing formation documents with the state called Articles of Incorporation or Certificate of Incorporation. Both have shareholders, directors, and officers. Both offer shareholders (owners) limited liability protection, meaning shareholders or owners are usually not responsible personally for business debts and legal liabilities. And both follow corporate processes and formalities to maintain the corporate entity. These can include adopting bylaws, issuing stock, holding shareholder and director meetings, and filing annual reports.

On the money side, personal income tax is due from you for any salary or dividends stemming from the company. But only an S corp has taxes passed through it, meaning the entity itself is not paying federal income taxes. A C corp must pay federal income taxes. An S corp is restricted to up to 100 shareholders, and all shareholders must be U.S. citizens and residents. A C corp has unrestricted ownership.

There is no way to tell you precisely what benefits you'll have as a DBA or an LLC or an S or C corp because there are so many variables based on your type of business, potential liability, plans for your company's future, taxation issues, and even where your business is located or conducted. A lawyer could easily tell you, within an hour of speaking with you about your business, which entity would be optimal for you. One more reason to hire a lawyer, if only for one hour!

Now that you have definitions and specifications coming out of your ears, here are two important things to remember:

- If you hire independent contractors to perform work for your business, or if you decide to take on employees or you are going to partner with someone, you should form an LLC or corporation.
- If you're solo and not incorporating your business in any other form, your legal business entity is a sole proprietorship. And remember you can use a DBA as a legal business name for your sole proprietorship, but it is not the actual entity for your business. (Always check with a lawyer and accountant in your state for the best advice).

Forming a corporation — either an S corp or C corp — is less common for most home-based businesses, especially ones that are small and not preparing for massive growth. A company with any other legal structure could always explore converting to one of the two corporation types in the future if the business is getting larger and more complex, with potentially more legal issues.

Sometimes the most prudent thing to do when faced with a lot of jargon and legalese is to turn to your trusted lawyer, and we did just that for our own businesses.

Danielle's legal stuff

When I first ventured into the wonderful world of " I-will-certainly-start-my-own-business," the actual business mumbo-jumbo was just that . . . foreign-sounding phrases I chose to ignore. You are reading this book because you are smarter than that, and you would like to learn from my mistakes. Aliza and I are all about saving you time and money. Once I decided I needed to make my business "official," I operated as a sole proprietorship. After researching further during the writing of this book, I began to understand that an LLC would provide an additional layer of protection, so in the interest of protecting my family "just in case," it's now an SMLLC.

Aliza's legal stuff

By the time you read this, I'll have established an SMLLC or Single Member LLC to replace the DBA that I was running for about six months. The main reason for doing this, for me at least, was peace of mind to know that if any legal action were to be taken against my company, my personal assets — and family assets — would be protected. I wasn't really anticipating anything bad happening; however, I am working more and more with independent contractors, so I am heeding the adage "better safe than sorry." I also consulted my bookkeeper, my tax accountant, and my lawyer, who all agreed that an LLC wasn't essential but was prudent, given the way my business is growing.

Let's Talk Taxes

According to the IRS, if you are a sole proprietor — including an independent contractor, a partner in a partnership, a member of a multi-member limited liability company (LLC), owner of an S corporation, or are otherwise in business for yourself — you usually must pay self-employment tax. This is not necessary if you have a C corp.

When should you make these payments? First, you need to know that these tax payments are typically called estimated quarterly tax payments. In her book *For the Love of Money*, Shannon King Nash explains when you must pay the IRS:

> "In general, you must make these estimated tax payments if you will owe $1,000 or more in taxes beyond your payroll tax withholdings. The amount of your estimated tax payments must be at least 90 percent of the taxes you will owe this year, 100 percent of your taxes from the previous year, or if your adjusted gross income is over $150,000, 110 percent of the previous year's taxes."

Your tax accountant or even bookkeeper can help you with your business taxes, but here's an important thing you need to know:

> You should file taxes four times a year, hence the "quarterly" in estimated quarterly tax payments.

Yes, you heard us right. These payments are calculated by looking at your net profits and estimating the taxes you'll owe. You or your bookkeeper or accountant can make these payments on the 15th of these months: April, June, September, and then January of the following year.

Why does the IRS make you do this? Shannon explains: "Because without this rule, self-employed folks wouldn't have to make these payments until they filed their tax returns. Keep in mind, most people who are employees are making tax payments every two weeks through their paycheck withholdings."

Phew! Now you see why we love our bookkeepers and accountants! If you had employees, you'd need to add a lot more steps to this process. Being a sole proprietor can help simplify an otherwise complicated process, although "simple" is clearly relative. You can visit MomIncorporated.com for links to handy calculators and further explanations about what you need to do in terms of taxes for your new business.

Getting an EIN

Employers with employees, business partnerships, and corporations must obtain an employer identification number (EIN) from the Internal Revenue Service. The EIN is also known as the Federal Tax Identification Number. You can get an EIN online in less than ten minutes through the IRS Web site (www.irs.gov) or by filling out the IRS Form SS-4.

You can also get an EIN for your business — even if it is a DBA. You don't have to be incorporated to file for an EIN. In fact, if you have or plan to have employees somewhere down the line, you definitely want to get an EIN. If you're a sole proprietor (DBA) and choose not to get an EIN, then you must use your personal Social Security number for tax dealings. So we say, get an EIN because it is always good to keep business separate from personal, even when it is just you in the company.

Before we move on from taxes and IRS-related topics, there are two important forms you might need to get from the IRS for your business: 1099 and W2 forms. The W2 form is used to report wages, salaries, and tips you've made to the IRS as an employee of a company. Generally, employers take taxes out of paychecks. In this case, your company takes out the taxes and pays them to the IRS throughout the year at every pay period. Those taxes are then reported on a W2 form.

The 1099 form is for income other than wages, salaries, and tips that can include income from work as an independent contractor. Employers do not take out taxes for an independent contractor. Instead, independent contractors must pay their own taxes, typically in quarterly tax payments. If you are an employee of your business and your business is incorporated, you should receive a W2 form for your salary. If you are working independently for a variety of clients, they will most likely provide you with a 1099 form.

Your bookkeeper, accountant, or payroll processing company can help you make sense of these forms if you need clarification.

Getting a Business License

Before you start doing business, it is a good idea to check to see if you need a business license. This can be specific to your town or city, your state, or nationally, depending on what you do and where you're based. You can find a handy searchable database on the Web, created by the Small Business Administration (SBA), called the Business License and Permit Search Tool, at http://www.sba.gov/licenses-and-permits. It provides a breakdown of federal, state, and local permits, licenses, and registrations you might need to do business in your area. Just enter your city, state, or zip code to access location-specific information and choose your business type to narrow down results.

Results are pretty straightforward. They provide you with the specific steps required to properly set up your business in your particular state, with links to relevant state agencies where you can get the paperwork and help you need.

While not all results from a search on SBA's Business License and Permit Search Tool will pertain to you, the site gives you a useful starting point to know what questions to ask and where you might go to get those answers. Always remember that the specifics to setting up your business properly can depend on where you live and are doing business, as well as the type of business you are forming.

AT-A-GLANCE GRID: Permitting Options

Here is a quick grid of the types of permits and where you might go to get them:

Permit Type	Where to Go?	You'll Probably Need If . . .
Tax Registration	IRS	You're going into business.
Business License	Dept. of Commerce or state business licensing division	You're going into business.
Building Permit	City or county building and planning department	You are constructing or modifying your place of business.
Health Permit	City or county health department	There is a lot of human contact taking place at your home-based business. Ex: In-home day care, anything health related. Also anything food related, but this is much more complicated if based in your home.
Occupational Permit	City or county building and planning development department	You're a home-based business in certain areas. Double-check this one!
Signage Permit	City or county building and planning department	You are going to literally hang a sign outside your home — some areas require a permit before you can do this.
Alarm Permit	City or county police or fire department	If you plan to install a burglar or fire alarm, you might need an alarm permit. Keep in mind this may apply if you have employees or other people coming to your place of business (your home) rather than if you are working solo and have valuable equipment to protect. This might also be required by your home or renters' insurance agency.
Zoning Permit	City or county building and planning department	You are developing land for commercial use. Running a business that requires objects to be placed on the land around your home, such as big signs in your yard? Yeah, you'd better check on what you can and cannot do in terms of zoning.

Getting Insurance

To get the low-down on insurance for home-based businesses, we turned to Jacquelyn Lynn, business writer and author of the e-book, *Get Covered: Business Insurance Made Simple*. Jacquelyn says the first thing you should do when thinking about insurance is to check your homeowners' or renters' insurance policy. There is a good chance that either may already cover a certain amount of business property. If it does, you need to think about whether or not the amount is sufficient.

Make a list of the property and items owned by your business, and estimate how much each thing is worth. Keep in mind that business property isn't just your computer and electronic equipment but also furniture. If you are making products, you should also include your specialized equipment and supplies and the product inventory you have on hand.

If your business property is worth $15,000 but your homeowners' insurance only covers $10,000, you need to decide if it is worth paying hundreds of dollars a year in premiums to cover a small number of items. You can better answer this question by doing a risk assessment that includes looking at your home security system as well as things like smoke alarms. You can even ask your local police department to provide you with a security assessment. Also consider your location and any associated risks from outside influences (potential theft or vandalism) or natural occurrences (storms, flooding, etc.).

If you're looking for more insurance, find a local insurance agent to discuss your needs. You can start with the agent who helped you with your homeowners' insurance, and see if he or she knows anything about insuring home-based businesses. You can also check with your local Chamber of Commerce or professional network to find someone to help you.

Marla Schulman, owner of brand consultancy Dvin/Ideas, was able to get liability coverage through her homeowners' insurance against accidents if she has meetings in her house. She also got a special insurance rider for her computer equipment with a $50 deductible and full coverage.

"I use computers for my work, so if one is stolen, or breaks, or blows up, I would need to replace it immediately with the same one. I have insured myself to have the ability to go out and replace it the same day," explains Marla. The cost? Only $18 extra per year, and Marla says that is a bargain for the peace of mind she gets, considering her computer is a $2,200 piece of equipment. She was with a friend recently who spilled coffee on her own computer and destroyed it.

"If it were mine, I would have been covered," says Marla.

"Don't over-insure, don't buy more coverage than you need," says Jacquelyn. "If you have a loss, the carrier is only going to pay for the actual loss. So if your equipment and inventory is worth $20,000, don't bother insuring it for $30,000. If you have inventory that fluctuates in value, talk to your agent about the best way to handle that; insurance carriers have policies that consider that."

In addition to insuring tangible things, you may need liability insurance, and that can be pricey. If you are making products where there is even a remote risk of being sued, it is better for you to be safe rather than sorry. This will be an expense you should build into your costs when planning out your business. If you are using or reselling products from other vendors, you may also want to have a copy of their insurance on hand.

For services companies, you could have liability if your customers ever come to your home to meet. Jacquelyn says you can avert this risk by holding meetings off-site, such as at your local coffee shop, rather than paying a lot for liability insurance.

Jacquelyn also recommends reading your policy or at least making sure you understand your deductibles, limitations, and other important details about your insurance. Find out what you need to do to comply with your insurance policy as well — such as saving invoices, receipts, and other records — in case you ever need to file a claim or defend yourself against a lawsuit. A good lawyer along with a good insurance agent can guide you through the process of assessing and managing your home-based business risks.

Moms Know Best

There is a ton of FREE help out there, including the SBA, and others. Check with your local university — they usually have a business center that can help and, better yet, some students who can [help you] as a class project!

—Susan Yniguez, Who's Your Mommy, LLC

Chapter 4
Show Me the Money

Now we're going to dive into the deep end of business planning. We want you to start thinking about money. In Chapter 1, we took you through some exercises to help you focus on the amount of money you wanted or needed to make, so your home based business would be the right kind of business for you. Now we're going to take you deeper into the money side of starting a business. Don't worry! We've got your back, plus a virtual life jacket for this part of your business adventure.

If you're a numbers kind of woman, you're probably going to breeze right through this chapter. If you're like us and prefer the creative side of having a business, we get it. Our best advice to you if the numbers part of starting your company doesn't send you into a state of bliss is "don't sweat it." This is where your A-Team comes into the picture, like a light at the end of a dark tunnel to guide you to understanding. Or at least to get you to a place where you are confident that your company financials are in good shape. Think of your bookkeeper and accountant especially as fitness trainers for your financials!

Crunching the Numbers

The following technical portion of our program on business financials could not have been written without the incredible guidance of Carol Roth, business strategist and *New York Times* best-selling author of *The Entrepreneur Equation*.

So Carol, where do we begin?

"You can take a top-down or bottom-up approach when you're thinking about your company's numbers," says Carol. "You can start with, 'I want to make $50,000 per year' — a financial goal — then work your way backwards. Or you can say, 'Here is realistically what I can do,' then flesh out what that looks like."

Here's what this looks like, taking a top-down approach:

I want to make $50,000 revenue a year.

I will charge $50 per hour.

$50,000 ÷ $50 = I will have to work 1,000 hours to reach my goal at the end of a year.

$50,000 ÷ 12 = I will have to make $4,160 per month to reach my goal.

$4,160 ÷ 4 = I'll have to sell $1,040 each week to reach my goal.

$1,040 ÷ $50* = I will have to work at least 20.8 hours per week to reach my goal.
* Your hourly rate

Is working on your business for 20 hours per week realistic? Start adding up your life equation: baby or children, partner, dinner, laundry, family activities, "Me" time, and of course, the unexpected. Are you at the right number?

If 20 hours is too much, something has got to shift. In your numbers crunching, it could be a smaller goal for annual revenues that will immediately reduce the amount of money you'll need to earn and number of hours you'll need to work to get to that goal. This is all just a rough estimate, of course, because this is not an exact science, and life — and business — can throw a lot of curve balls.

Now let's walk through this calculation, so you can start wrapping your head around your business financials:

State how much you want to make per year.	$_____ = SALES
How much do you plan to charge? Price per hour for services, price per item for product.	$_____ = PRICE
Divide the amount you want to make per year by your hourly rate (or price for product) to see how many hours you need to work — or items you need to sell — to reach this number.	SALES ÷ PRICE = AMOUNT YOU HAVE TO SELL/WORK #_____
Divide amount you want to make per year by 12 months to find out how much (ballpark) you need to make per month.	SALES ÷ 12 = MONTHLY SALES $_____
Divide this number by 4 (as in 4 weeks) to see how much you need to make weekly.	MONTHLY SALES ÷ 4 = WEEKLY SALES $_____
Divide that number by your hourly rate or per item price to see how many hours per week you have to work or items you have to sell to reach your annual revenue goal.	WEEKLY SALES ÷ PRICE = WEEKLY HOURS #_____

You can download this top-down calculation worksheet on MomIncorporated.com and print it out as many times as you need to work through your numbers.

Here is a worksheet filled in for a company calculating how many hours need to be worked (or items sold) based on sales goals and with a higher hourly rate or item price than the one used in the previous example ($100 per hour or item instead of $50):

State how much you want to make per year.	$50,000 = SALES
How much do you plan to charge? Price per hour for services, price per item for product.	$100 = PRICE
SALES ÷ PRICE = AMOUNT YOU HAVE TO SELL/WORK	500
SALES ÷ 12 = MONTHLY SALES	$4,160
MONTHLY SALES ÷ 4 = WEEKLY SALES	$1,040
WEEKLY SALES ÷ PRICE = WEEKLY HOURS	10.4

10.4 hours per week? Is that more realistic, at least to start?

Hire a bookkeeper (or accountant) before things start to get out of control. I used to go nuts around tax time trying to play catch-up. Accounting wasn't my core competency. I'd rather pay someone a little bit of money and save my sanity.

—Karla Trotman, BellyButtonBoutique.com

You also need to think of the time you will have to spend to market your company, to pitch and land new clients or gain new customers, and all the other things that running a business entails. But this calculation worksheet gives you numbers you can wrap your head around as you're thinking about what it's going to take to start your business.

Still not sure what your magic annual revenue number is or should be? Let's take a bottom-up approach and do some financial figuring that will help you come at this equation from a different angle: How much can you work, and what do you want to charge for it? Most important, does the time and money you've just indicated make sense?

Say you just can't realistically see working more than 10 hours per week, because 20 hours would definitely not work for you. Let's also say you want to charge $50 per hour.

10 hours x 4 weeks =	40 hours working per month
$50 x 40 hours =	$2,000 of income per month you can expect to generate at that rate.
$2,000 x 12 =	$24,000 is what you can expect to earn in a year, at that rate of pay and that number of work hours put into your company.

Is $24,000 a good number to you? If not, you can increase your price, increase the number of hours you intend to work, or both in order to increase that magic annual sales number.

You can download a handy bottom-up calculation worksheet on MomIncorporated.com. We recommend printing out both a top-down and bottom-up worksheet, and work with the one that makes the most sense to you.

For better cash flow: Don't offer "30 days credit" (or Net 30), which means clients would have 30 days to pay you. Ask for payment up front or on the day you deliver the goods or services. Or ask for a deposit. As soon as you issue an invoice, contact your client to check that they have received the invoice and that it is all in order.

—Heather Smith, ANISE Consulting

Understanding Business Financials

The numbers side of financials can be challenging, but the acronyms and terminology for financials can be downright confusing. So we've put together some quick definitions of common financial terms used in a standard business financial statement. Here they are:

Sales: The amount of money you bring in by selling products or services. This is the price (or fee) you are charging, multiplied by the number of products (or services) you've sold each month, multiplied by 12 months. Think of this as your big pool of money for the year. Important to note: This is not the actual money that goes into your pocket at the end of the year. This is a starting point. You then have to subtract your expenses to see what you have left that you can actually pocket.

Cost of Sales: Or Cost of Goods. This is considered "directly attributable costs." Translation? Anything that is specific to the thing you are selling but not the cost of running your business. For example, if you are selling cupcakes, this means the cost of the flour and the eggs but not the cost of your marketing efforts — those are business expenses. Here's another example: We are producing a book that will be published. The cost for publishing this book includes the cost of paper and printing — these are direct costs or Cost of Goods. But all the other things we spend producing the book — our time writing it, our time promoting it — are costs of doing business. Note: Service companies may not have any direct costs related to the services they offer.

Gross Margin: This number is the difference between Sales and Cost of Sales, so: SALES − COST OF SALES = GROSS MARGIN. If you had a restaurant, retail store, or were selling consumer products, you would need to make sure you're selling your goods for enough money to cover the overhead for running your business. Think of the Gross Margin as a checkpoint to double-check that you are pricing your product correctly. Service businesses have very few direct costs associated with them, so there is more money left over to run the business or a higher Gross Margin. Keep in mind that although service businesses could have a higher Gross Margin, they also could have higher labor costs; you are selling your time, your hours.

Overhead Expenses: This is the cost of running your business. In some cases, if you are selling services by the hour, paying a consultant could be an expense of running your business. Overhead Expenses cover all other things required to run your business (such as administrative costs, marketing, rent, utilities, etc.). It is a good idea to include all of these when you're evaluating your business financials. Administrative costs cover general management of your business and can include fees for bookkeeping, general legal work and accounting. What they don't include are marketing, manufacturing, or expenses directly related to sales. If you are planning to use your house rent as a business expense, please remember to first check with your CPA before you apply any household expenses as business ones.

Earnings Before Interest and Taxes (or EBIT): This is how much your business makes before your financing decisions and taxes come into play. This is the profit *your business* is making rather than how much *you* are making.

Earnings Before Interest, Taxes, Depreciation, and Amortization (or EBITDA): Depreciated Assets are big items you purchase to run your business that lose value over time. This part may not be relevant to you if you haven't had to buy big pieces of equipment.

Interest: Have you had to finance your business by taking on debt, such as getting a loan from the bank? If so, taking on debt means you will be making interest payments every month.

Taxes Incurred: This depends on your tax bracket. Check with your CPA.

Net Profit: This is the number on paper that tells you what you've made from your business. This number does not account for *how* you assign that money, such as whom you pay and when. Also, if someone doesn't pay you on time, that isn't reflected in the Net Profit number either until they pay you, since "net" tells you what you've actually made. From a financial accounting standpoint, this is what you could be "taking home" as your income from your business. Consider this number your "sanity check" to make sure you are on the right track and making enough money from your business.

To add a little twist to business financials, keep in mind that your accountant will look at your company finances on a cash basis. This means that if you sold a product in December but you weren't paid until January, it will show up in your company's financial records as December income but in your tax records as January income.

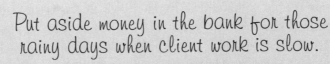

Put aside money in the bank for those rainy days when client work is slow.

—Laurie Juliano, LL Bach & Associates

Here's what the financial terms from pages 95–96 look like in an Income Statement:

Revenue	FY 2011	FY 2012
Sales	$	$
Direct Cost of Sales	$	$
Other Costs of Sales	$	$
Total Cost of Sales	$	$
Gross Margin	$	$
Gross Margin %	%	%
Expenses	$	$
Payroll	$	$
Marketing/Promotion	$	$
Rent	$	$
Utilities	$	$
Insurance	$	$
Payroll Taxes	$	$
Other	$	$
Total Operating Expenses	$	$
Earnings Before Interest and Taxes	$	$
EBITDA	$	$
Interest Expense	$	$
Taxes Incurred	$	$
Net Profit	$	$
Net Profit/Sales %	%	%

Whew! We've covered a lot of hard ground here. Now let's talk about where you can get the money you need to start, run, and grow your new home-based business. There are a lot of options, and we'll explain many of the most common ones and provide our recommendations, as well as advice from women who have received funding in one form or another.

Meeting Your Capital Needs

"Capital Needs" means the money you must have to get your business off the ground. How much money do you really need to start — and run — your business? We've helped you work through numbers in several different ways. Once you've seen your "magic number" in writing, you need to think more about how you'll cover the costs of your business. Can you cover those costs yourself? Or will you have to turn somewhere else for the money?

In Chapter 2, we gave you a number of examples of Web-based businesses you could start for relatively low start-up costs, from several hundred dollars to a few thousand. Do you have enough money to cover those costs? If not, where will that money come from?

Here is a list of some funding sources for companies:

Self-funding. This is one of the most common ways businesses get started — the founder of the business funds it out of personal savings. In some cases, entrepreneurs might use their credit cards to fund their business. Everyone will tell you the same thing: Bad idea. Take out a home equity loan? Bad idea. Until you have a proven business track record, try not to do anything that jeopardizes the financial well-being of your family and household.

Spouse/Partner. Your life partner is in it for the long haul, so he or she should be a great source of income for your business, right? Not necessarily. If you are starting a business to help bring in money for your household, your partner may not have any wiggle room to spare the extra cash. Sure, you could make a persuasive argument for using your joint savings or that vacation fund you've both contributed to for your start-up costs. But do you really want to go down that path? You may get the money you need in the short term, but those actions could breed resentment in your home over the long haul. We aren't saying don't ask. We're just saying be careful.

Family member. A relative other than your spouse or partner might be a possibility; however, turning to family members for capital for your business can be fraught with emotional baggage. That said, many businesses have been started and run initially on what is commonly known as a "Friends and Family" round of financing. Even if someone is your favorite aunt or beloved grandparent, make sure you put everything in writing and that you both agree to the terms and know what you are getting into. This is a good time to get a lawyer involved — even with family.

Sara Macias started her fashion design company from home when her son was 3 years old. She funded her company with $1,200 left over from her college fund and purchased fabrics, cutting tables, notions, organizational bins, and business cards. When she was seeking $1,000 to create a line of clothes to sell at a major convention, she began working up a business plan to get a bank loan, asking her mother for advice as she wrote. Finally, her mother offered to cover the $1,000 as a no-interest loan.

"I have borrowed money from my mother in the past before," says Sara, "so it was just a verbal agreement that I will pay her back when the time comes, which I will, of course."

Sara was lucky — and so was her mom. Sara has a history of paying back loans to her mom which is great, but we can't recommend going into any agreement with anyone — even family — without a written agreement. While it may seem unnecessary, getting into the habit of putting everything into writing — even a one- or two-page "Memorandum of Understanding" or MOU signed by both parties — can create the clarity and reassurance everyone needs to have a more stress-free transaction. You can visit MomIncorporated.com for more information on MOUs, something you can draft on your own or with the help of a lawyer.

"My mother is very good with money and is in a good position to loan money and wait that long for payment back," says Sara. "I honestly wouldn't take anyone's money — family, friends, etc., if I knew borrowing money from them would be risky for both parties."

Sara also advises that you know exactly what you're borrowing the money for and how much you need. "Being a good businessperson is knowing what your costs are. Don't go blindly asking for too much or too little, thinking you know it all."

Keep your business and personal finances separate. It sounds simple, but you need to be very diligent in these efforts. Have a separate bank account for your business income and expenses. Since the money you make is your "income," transfer a portion as your self-appointed "salary" into your personal account when you receive payment for your work, and leave the rest in your business account for "operating expenses."

—Christie Glascoe Crowder, ChatterBox Christie

Friend. This is the other half of the "Friends and Family" round. Yes, they are your BFFs, and they might even be rich, and the money you need could be a drop in the proverbial bucket to them. But consult a lawyer and put everything in writing if you're going to go this route to fund your business. Anytime people give you money, you have to be clear if they are giving you an interest-free loan, a low-interest loan, or if you don't have to pay them back but they expect to own a piece of your company. This begins to get more complicated as you move to angel investors or venture capitalists.

Bank loan. With the economy at a lower point than it has been in years, and with many banks in hot water, getting a bank loan may be tougher than ever. In the past, it has been very difficult for woman-owned companies to obtain loans and other funding. Rather than go into the politics of bank loans to women, we can say there are newer creative ways to fund your business, and we outline some of those later in this book. If you attempt to get a loan from a bank, you'll need to have your business plan and financials totally buttoned up. A good accountant and a great banker can help you work through the possible financing options from banks for your company, including a line of credit, which is a preestablished amount of money that you can borrow against as needed, or a loan guaranteed by the Small Business Administration (SBA). You can also turn to your Small Business Development Center (SBDC) or the SBA directly to identify financing options and assistance.

According to Maria Coyne, Executive Vice President of Business Banking at Key Bank, some of the types of financing that business owners can get through a bank such as Key include term loans, leases, lines of credit, credit cards, and government-guaranteed products. There are similar products on the personal banking side that are often leveraged by the business owner for their business.

"Frequently, home-based business owners merely start with personal savings or equity investments from family and friends," says Maria. "If they do take on debt, they are also often leveraging a home equity loan, a loan from a retirement account, or a credit card."

If you're looking to get a bank loan for your home-based business, Maria advises that you "maintain detailed financial records and use those financial reports — your income statement, cash projections, balance sheet, receivables/payables, etc. — to run your business. You need to demonstrate an understanding of the cash inflows and outflows from your business."

In terms of funding your business, Maria says to begin conservatively and always assume you'll need more of a "cushion" than you originally anticipated. Run "worst case" scenarios to ensure that you understand how much cash will be needed on hand to keep your business afloat during tough times. Keep a handle on ramping up fixed expenses too quickly.

As you start thinking about working with a bank, it is important to find a banker who is going to listen and get to know your business before he or she starts suggesting solutions. Pick someone who is going to work with you as your partner for the long haul and is willing to build a relationship. Part of this involves honesty on both sides, as well as a shared goal around the success of the business.

Look for referrals to banks and bankers from friends, colleagues, and other business owners. Even your bookkeeper, accountant, or lawyer may have a good relationship with a banker and can make a referral. If you have a banker you trust whom you've dealt with on your personal or home finances, ask him or her to refer you to someone within the branch who specializes in business banking.

Even when you have an excellent relationship with a bank, that's no guarantee of getting a business loan. Wendy Ambruster Bell of Snugabell Mom & Baby Gear says she ran into a cash flow challenge early on in her business and turned to a variety of personal banking tools to keep things going.

"Everything was funded on lines of credits and credit cards until two years in, when my husband and I refinanced our mortgage because our bank of 25 years wouldn't lend us any money based on our business plan," Wendy recalls.

The good news is her company didn't have to touch the operating line of credit that she and her husband got by refinancing their mortgage. The company's cash flow finally improved and her sales increased by more than 150 percent over the previous year. Things were certainly looking up from there!

What About Credit Cards?

We're not ones to recommend racking up credit card debt. We've both done it, and we know a lot of women who have done it, but you have to have a lot of self-discipline to prevent your spending from spinning out of control. Lahronda Little knows about this kind of debt. She started her company, High Quality Organic Skincare LLC, using her own money —including savings — then ran off her earnings for a while.

"I got to a point where I needed more money and didn't want to deplete my savings," says Lahronda, who decided to use the credit tools offered by Paypal and Amazon. A lot of her business transactions were already processed through Paypal, including vendor payments, raw materials, and printed materials, so she began using Paypal's Smart Connect as an option for additional money. She then applied for Amazon credit and purchased the small-scale manufacturing items she needed.

Paypal's Smart Connect functions like a credit card and is different from the main PayPal money service. Both Smart Connect and Amazon's credit card are run through GE Money, and the finance fees are steep — about 26.99 percent. Lahronda cringes at the thought of those exorbitant fees but says both money sources were readily available to her just when she needed them, so she used them. She says she spent about $1,500 total on the high-interest credit loans and is adamant about keeping her debt down. She also believes she will pay off the debt quickly — within three months' time.

We caution anyone who is considering going for the fast and "easy" money that comes with large finance fees. It is all too common for this kind of debt to build faster than one can pay it. Lahronda is aware of the possible dangers of her financing methods and takes a bit of a "do as I say, not as I do" approach in her advice:

"As much as possible, use your own funding or from family or friends," Lahronda recommends. "Do not use credit unless you can generate enough income to pay it off very quickly. The worst thing in the world would be to start a business that does not work out and then be shackled with debt."

Running off Client Revenues

An ideal way to start a home-based business is with a client or some customers already lined up. If you left your job to have a baby and then decided not to go back to the 9-to-5 grind, start with approaching your previous employer — not with a letter of resignation, but instead with an offer to provide consulting work as an independent consultant. Any savvy business owner knows the savings on paying employee benefits when working with an independent contractor. Your offer might be too good for them to refuse, and you'll land your first client! Check with a legal adviser or accountant to carefully review rules surrounding working as an independent contractor to make sure your arrangement with your former employer is in compliance with the IRS.

Kathy Zucker, owner of the strategic marketing firm, Zucker Productions, LLC, suffered some health-related setbacks following the birth of her baby and was hesitant to return to her marketing job at a hospital after her maternity leave was coming to an end. After discussing her options with her husband, the couple agreed that she could stay home and continue working with the hospital as a consulting client. The hospital signed on as Kathy's first client, and soon after she signed two more clients. Revenues from those clients kept her business running, and she eventually expanded her clientele to service other industries, including real estate.

Kathy says she has one ironclad business rule that helps her continue to run off client revenues: "I never ever spend more on childcare than I'm making and can afford to pay."

Having seen other moms with home-based businesses pay far more for childcare than their revenues can cover, Kathy says she is careful not to get into the same financial bind. Childcare can be expensive, but it shouldn't bankrupt your business before it gets off the ground. The revenue Kathy generates through her company now affords her the ability to cover childcare, so she can work 20 to 25 hours per week.

Get Money, Creatively

Even with the many traditional ways of raising money for our businesses, some moms try ontirely different money-raising tactics with good results. Miko Franklin, mother of a three-year-old, started her public relations company, The Publicity Stunt, Inc., in her home and raised funds using . . . Facebook.

"I used a fundraising tool on Facebook — FundRazr," Miko explains. "The tool is typically used by nonprofits, but it did help me to raise all the funding I needed to establish my parent company as an LLC and get started with my Web site."

Miko calculated that she needed to raise about $1,000 for fees to form her LLC and to pay a Web developer to get her Web site off the ground. Using the FundRazr app, she was able to send out messages to her Facebook friends asking for their support. About 50 people contributed to her cause. She originally wanted to ask for $1 because she thought that if each of her 1,000 Facebook friends could contribute a dollar, she'd have enough money to get started. The FundRazr app, however, was set at a minimum donation of $5. While not all of her Facebook friends contributed, some did put in $20, $50, even $100.

She exceeded her goal and paid the $500 fee in Illinois to establish her LLC, then put the balance toward Web site design and development.

Says Miko, "I thanked those who contributed by sending them individualized 'thank you' messages, tagging them in posts in which I expressed my thanks, and continuously posting general messages thanking those who believed in me enough to provide financial support for my business venture."

Talk about creative funding! There are also services online called "crowdfunding" sites where you can use Web-based and social network–based tools to solicit funds from both people you know and even the general public. Crowdfunding is an aspect of crowdsourcing, where you use online tools to reach out quickly and easily to many people to ask them to contribute relatively small amounts of money toward a project. Because many people end up participating, the cumulative amount of money can be significant. You can check out sites like Profounder.com, Invested.in, and Kickstarter.com to see if they might be useful to help you raise money to build your home-based business. Profounder and Invested.in are geared toward entrepreneurs, while Kickstarter is geared more toward creative projects, funding films, art installations, music recordings, book publishing, and product prototypes.

Going for the Big Bucks

We've covered a lot of ways to fund your company, but there are still a few more strategies that involve doing a lot more work, both to prepare yourself and your company to approach people with money. Big money.

Up to now, we've asked you a lot of questions about your motivations for starting a business, your passions, and your vision. We've tried to be straight with you about the challenges of starting a business from home, particularly if you have a baby or are about to have a baby, or even if you have young children still at home. We've especially trie[d] not taking on too much too quickly, in order to create a manageable work/li[fe] yourself — and your family.

But we would never be ones to discourage you from doing something bigger, the gusto, from Going Big or Going Home. Do you want to build an empire? Go f[or] that once you decide to go for the big money, you put yourself on a trajectory big time, and it will take a lot of time, energy, determination, and sacrifice to [?]

Are you ready for that? Even if you aren't right this moment, let us tell you about some other ways to get bigger money to take your company to the next level and beyond. Information is power! Here are some additional funding sources you can seek out.

Angel funding. Angel funding comes from an angel investor, an individual with the means to invest both his or her own money and often other resources (such as skills and contacts) to help start-up companies get off the ground. Angels often like to roll up their sleeves and be helpful in launching a company. They are taking big risks in newer businesses ,so they also get more equity in a company for less money, meaning they will get a larger percentage ownership of a company at a lower cost than later investors. You can find angels through your personal and professional networks or, more likely, through contacts whom your network knows. You can also find these early-stage investors through angel lists and groups, located easily on the Web through a Google search for "angel investor networks."

Or contact the SBA to access the list they maintain of general angel investors, including some who focus on woman-led companies. We also include a list of links to resources on MomIncorporated.com.

Finding an angel investor can happen in many ways, and landing one will make a difference in what you do with your company. Take Lisa Cottrell-Bentley as an example. After over eight years trying to become a published author, Lisa finally decided to launch her own independent publishing company called Do Life Right, Inc. Her vision was to produce books depicting realistic homeschoolers, to reach the homeschooling market. Lisa, herself, was homeschooling her two young daughters.

She decided she wanted to seek outside funding. She did her homework, put together a business plan and a marketing plan, and compiled six unedited but complete book manuscripts. Then she went searching for an angel investor.

Where did she go to find investors? Lisa was lucky enough to have made contacts in the venture capital world while helping her husband seek funding for his software company, so she had access to people who were interested in investing in companies. Within a month of queries, she found a first-time investor, a woman, who believed in Lisa's vision.

Lisa's investor committed $15,000 to her publishing company: $8,000 up front, and then $2,000 to $3,000 increments every month or so. How did she use the money? Lisa trademarked a logo, bought ISBNs (identifier codes for individual books) and LCCNs (Library of Congress cataloguing numbers) for the books she would publish, paid a designer for illustrations and cover designs for two of her books, covered the printing costs for those books, and paid for some marketing materials, including banners and Web sites. She even had enough to buy books about editing and to attend a related conference.

"Even with my very detailed plan of how things would work if I received the money, what actually happened was much different," admits Lisa. "The initial plan was that the money would pay for publishing three books, but it didn't work out that way."

Instead, the proceeds from the sales of her first two books were enough to cover the costs of publishing two additional books in her own book series and three books by other authors. She has since signed on 12 additional authors, with six more books scheduled for publication. Not too bad a result from an initial $15,000 investment.

The amount Lisa's angel investor put into her company is smaller than typical angel investments, which average around $25,000, says Stephanie Hanbury-Brown, managing director of Golden Seeds, an angel investor group and venture capital fund. Some individual angel investors do invest in the $100,000 to $200,000 range; however, more will often invest under $100,000.

What motivates a person to become an angel investor? Stephanie says the reasons vary, but in her experience, she sees individuals who have had their own success as entrepreneurs and are looking to stay involved with innovation or to give back by supporting other entrepreneurs. Angels can invest in companies as individual investors or participate together to make a larger investment, more in the range of $500,000 to $2 million. Anything higher than that is usually the territory of venture capitalists.

Venture capital. Venture capital comes from venture firms, entities with pooled resources and money coming from a variety of sources. A venture capitalist or VC works at a venture firm, and brokers deal with high-growth start-ups, usually investing millions of dollars at a time. While angel investors typically put in money early in the life of a company, venture capitalists more often wait until after an angel round happens before then considering investing.

Stephanie explains that one main difference between an angel investor and a venture capitalist is that the angel investor is investing his or her own money, while a VC is investing other people's money. Right off the bat, the VC has an obligation to his or her fund to make a sound investment and make money from it. So what does this mean for you, the entrepreneur?

An angel will write you a check because he or she believes in you and your business idea and genuinely wants to help you grow your company. The VC is looking to do everything it takes to grow your company quickly, even if it means ousting you as head of the company if he or she feels you can't cut the mustard and meet high growth goals. Angel investors would like to make money in the long run off their investment but tend to be less aggressive about it. Venture capitalists have a keen eye on the "exit strategy," which usually means either selling your company or "going public" in an IPO (Initial Public Offering) so their investors can make a lot of money and move on to the next deal. This is the big time, baby. Go Big or Go Home!

One woman we know and admire who is Going Big is Laura "@Pistachio" Fitton, coauthor of *Twitter for Dummies.* Her entrepreneurial story started when she was a recently separated single mom with two toddlers. She had a home-based consulting company focused on marketing businesses on Twitter when she came up with the idea for a Web-based company called oneforty. She named her company as a reference to the 140 characters allowed in a tweet on Twitter.

Laura's business started out as a Web site with reviews and links to Twitter consumer apps, and she soon began seeking funding to take her business to the next level. During this time, she was accepted to Tech Stars, an intense start-up accelerator program that helps entrepreneurs gain access to resources, mentors, and funding to grow their companies. After many meetings and negotiations, Laura surpassed her initial fundraising goals by nearly $100,000 when she raised $235,000 from angel investors. She then obtained a second angel round of $150,000 before closing her first venture round of $1.9 million six months later.

Why did investors take a chance on Laura's company? To start, her passion was infectious, and she displayed the perseverance to lead the company. She also demonstrated to potential investors an expertise in using Twitter for business — building her profile this way helped her to gain their trust. But Laura didn't do all of this alone.

"We had assembled a small, powerful team that was executing like crazy," says Laura.

Her investors were also excited about the tremendous potential for building a big company, because oneforty was creating tools and resources related to Twitter, which was experiencing skyrocketing growth at that time. Since then, oneforty has expanded beyond just Twitter to be a social business hub and buyer's guide for businesses seeking digital tools and strategies.

Laura, like most entrepreneurs who seek funding from angels and VCs, knows the sacrifices it takes to be a true entrepreneur. As one example, she recalls the three months she spent away from her children, only seeing them on Skype each night, as she was working to build her company clear across the country.

Stephanie, from Golden Seeds, draws clear distinctions between a business owner who is looking for a lifestyle business — something flexible, something that can be done from home — and an entrepreneur who is willing to make the sacrifices, work the long hours, and do whatever it takes to grow something big and is only too happy to sell the company and then move on to the next one.

"Investors look for a really good entrepreneur with a big idea, something that is scalable," says Stephanie. "They look for an entrepreneur who has the ability to execute an idea. They look for a business that can become a multimillion-dollar company within several years. And they are looking for a clear exit strategy, so they can put their money in and get it back out again."

Aliza on money

I've started and run a number of businesses over the years. For my first company — an Internet business called Cybergrrl, Inc. — started in 1995, my business partner and I met with angel investors and venture capitalists and ended up receiving $300,000 in funding from a media company. Keep in mind that this wasn't a home-based business, and we had a team of over twenty creative people working on client services, such as Web development, Web hosting, and Internet marketing, as well as publishing our own Web sites, where we generated income from advertising and sponsorships and an e-mail list with over 40,000 women subscribing to our e-newsletter. Plus we ran an online and offline organization I started called Webgrrls International that had grown to over 100 chapters worldwide with 30,000 women participating.

After meeting with many angel investors and venture capitalists, a mentor of mine finally introduced us to a major, family-owned tech publishing company. The company saw great growth potential in our vision for educating and empowering women to get online and benefit from technology. They offered us $1 million in funding. Naively, we refused to take that much money, thinking that we'd lose control of our company. We agreed to take $300,000 so we wouldn't have to give up too much ownership of our business. We soon learned what a big mistake we made as we ran through the money far more quickly than we anticipated.

Since learning that tough lesson, I've run several Internet consulting businesses from home on my own and kept things small, usually using a credit card for small purchases, such as office supplies, until I was making enough money from client work to spend more money. I didn't turn anywhere else for funding because I wasn't interested in the stress and pressure of taking someone else's money.

In 2005, I incorporated my company and began bringing in over $100,000 a year, but when I applied for a bank loan for $15,000 to finance the purchase of some technical equipment, I was denied. I was still affected by the tremendous debt and financial fallout that occurred after I left my first Internet company, and it has taken me many years to fully recover from that tumultuous time. The bank simply looked at the surface of my financial records without delving further into the particulars of my situation.

Luckily, my husband was willing to cosign and personally guarantee the loan, and I was able to get a line of credit and a corporate credit card, although both were in his name. I paid back the loan in full over the next two years from the money I earned through consulting and writing books.

With my current home-based mobile strategy and apps development business, I'm operating off of the money I make from consulting clients, as well as some freelance income I receive from writing articles, blog posts, and books. Because my business is less than a year old, I've been unable to get a bank line of credit or corporate credit card for my company. I could get these if I guaranteed everything personally; however, I've learned some hard lessons about keeping business and personal money separate. So I just keep expenses low and manageable so I can operate off of what I earn. These days, I'm putting far more emphasis on having less financial stress and more time to spend with my family.

Have more start-up capital for the launch of a product than you think you'll need. You may put a lot of money into making the product professional and having a top-notch Web site, but allocate enough funds for advertising and marketing right from the start.

—Jill Leech, Potty Tots, LLC

Danielle on money

As I've previously mentioned, I decided to start ExtraordinaryMommy without a large investment. I didn't create an extensive business plan (Mistake #1), and I didn't put a cap on how much we — my family . . . this is a FAMILY investment — would choose to invest in this business venture (Mistake #2). ExtraordinaryMommy was created on, as they say, a "wing and prayer" — the faith and finances of our family — so that meant what my husband was actually earning and a lot of woman hours. What I didn't invest in cash, I invested in time.

My initial cash investment included the creation of the ExtraordinaryMommy Web site, Web hosting, and the logo, for which I paid dearly. I didn't do the appropriate research, which would have shown me that I could have commissioned a Web site header for less than $100 (maybe even less than $50). I paid $800. You know what this means? The logo for ExtraordinaryMommy.com will never, ever change. It is a good thing I love it.

Are you tallying my mistakes? I'm fortunate that my overall expenditures were minor: I didn't have any employees, no outside office, no fax machine. That isn't to say I didn't invest — that WE didn't invest in the business — but I didn't take out a loan to get it started. There is easily as much sweat equity invested in my business as actual dollars.

It was a full two and a half years of working long hours and investing personally in this business before I saw a profit. I operate from the money I earn from consulting and being hired as a correspondent, from video work, media training, and writing. My biggest expenses come in the form of travel, as I consider it a priority to network with like-minded people at events such as BlissDom, BlogHer, Type A Mom, and

The Evolution of Women in Social Media (EVO) conferences. I have continued to make valuable connections and increase my work opportunities, but I believe I have to invest in myself if I expect others to be willing to invest in me.

Since the beginning of 2010, I have realized one of my initial goals: to contribute financially to my family. I am now responsible for a portion of our monthly expenses. Success. My next goal? Making enough to give my husband the freedom to choose a career he loves.

Going for OPM (Other People's Money)

If you seek outside funding for your company, remember two very important things:

1. Once you go to someone else for money, you create new pressures for yourself in terms of hitting financial goals in your business.

2. If you are really hoping to stay home based, most people will not want to risk giving you money when you're limiting their possibility of making bigger money off their investment in you.

We're not saying you can't take the pressure. Maybe you can, although we'll always be the first to say that if you are staying home with small children, especially a newborn, external pressures — namely financial ones — are simply not a good idea.

Also, we are definitely not saying to avoid planning for a big successful company. But let's be honest: Big successful companies are not often run by stay-at-home moms with little ones running around who require time and attention throughout the day. That isn't at all to say it cannot be done — and in Chapter 8 we do introduce you to some awesome women who have had big success — but it tends to be the exception, not the rule.

We want you to be successful — and not just at business, but in all the many facets of your work and your life. We'll just keep reminding you to think long and hard about what you want, so you can be at your best and feel good about what you're doing.

Chapter 5
A Room of Your Own

We understand that as you wrap your brain around your new business venture, you have a lot to think about. Hopefully, we've helped lay out some steps to push you to put your plans on paper and make a list of each task you need to tackle. Soon you'll need to spread your wings as you not only mentally make time for this new chapter in your life and decide what type of company to start, but as you actually make space in your home for this new endeavor.

Much like there are spaces in your home for specific uses, your business will require a "location" of its own. You need to have a "place" in your home that allows the ideas to flow freely, the paperwork to stay organized, and the work to get done. Where could you put your home office? You could convert a seldom-used guest room, a corner of your basement, or even — as many moms have discovered — the kitchen counter or dining room table. For the best results and most productivity, we recommend setting up a "fixed space" or one that doesn't force you to pack up your office equipment every time your family sits down to a meal. Maybe a corner of your kitchen can be converted into a workspace, or you could clear a pantry to tuck away your work equipment and supplies.

Having your own space will allow you to draw that definitive line between the work you do as a mom and the work you do as a business owner. Plus, your kids need room to play. So do you. Regardless of where you get creative with space, look for a bit of permanence to give your business some stability from the get-go. You'll get more done, and there'll be less disruption for both you and your family. Having dedicated space for each in your life will allow you to be the BEST mom and the BEST business owner possible.

Define Your Space

If your home is anything like ours, you can't hide the fact that children live there. Shelves are covered with books, board games and, in some cases, baseballs (because someone who-shall-remain-nameless decided "real balls" in the home are OK). Coloring books peek out of drawers, the odd sock sits atop a pillow on the couch, all in stark contrast to the image you had in your head when you used Pottery Barn catalogs to mentally decorate the space. Children take over everything, and it may feel as though there is nothing but a corner by the refrigerator left for the taking.

But this is important: you *need* space to work. It doesn't have to be huge, but it has to be yours, and it should fit your needs, your personality, and your work style.

Let's discuss your in-home options: A table. A corner. A room.

Really? Can you really run a business from your kitchen table or from your living room floor? Sure you can. Depending on the type of business you start, it isn't always necessary to have a big space, but it is important how you use the space. Your space is also defined by the rules you put into place with your family.

So many of us start our businesses on our kitchen tables. We drop our laptops down, whip out the files, the pens, the tricks of our individual trades, and before we know it, our families are juggling plates of spaghetti on their laps instead of sitting down to eat so they don't disturb Mommy's work. You can see how this might not work out for long. Having your "office" or "office space" out in the open can create challenges. You are constantly visible to your family, and the goings-on of your household are constantly visible to you. Oh wait, are those dishes that need to be done?

What suits your personality? Can you work with noise and small people around you? Do you prefer being in the midst of the chaos because it keeps your finger on the pulse of your family while running your business? Or do you need total silence because you have trouble staying focused once you've been interrupted?

Maybe you *want* to be out in the open to keep an eye on your kids. Maybe you need to be accessible and can easily answer to a cry for food or a "What's for dinner?" and "Mommy, can you tie this for me?" while responding to an e-mail and fulfilling an order. Or maybe the very thought of that sends you into a tizzy. Be honest about what you need, so you can set up the right workspace. There is no single correct way to make room for your business. If it works, it works — we're saying to just give it some careful thought.

Find a spot in your home you can call your own and that is somehow separate — even if it's just a desk that is specifically for your project.

—Jackie Ekholm, Moo Chocolates

Explore Your In-Home Options

Here are some quick things to think about when considering where to put your workspace. Is there a table in the house that isn't part of your family's everyday activities, one with enough surface space that would allow you to spread out and start working?

No? Then can you look in the attic, the basement, or the garage for one that may be collecting dust, and move it to a space in the house that suits your needs? We want to encourage you to keep your initial business expenses to a minimum, so try to get creative about finding a table somewhere that you can claim as your work desk. Maybe you can take one off a friend or family member's hands?

If you're coming up empty, look for an inexpensive solution. On craigslist, while we were writing this book, there were no less than a dozen tables or desks being offered in the St. Louis area (where Danielle lives) ranging from $40 to $150.

If you have an extra room for your home office, you are one lucky girl. This means a few things:

- You have room to spread out.
- You can go in and close the door.
- You can walk away and leave work behind you at the end of the day.
- You can really create a space that is not only efficient, but one that inspires your creative process.

CHEAT SHEET: The 3 Ps of a Suitable "Office Space"

Permanence. Ideally, you want to look for a permanent spot, one that does not have to be packed up and squirreled away each day.

Productivity. Your space may be small, but it has to have the items you need to maximize your productivity. You will need some basic office supplies, but beyond that, you might also need specific tools that apply to your chosen business. And don't forget to fulfill your emotional needs as well. Maybe you need an open window to keep your energy level high and your mind clear. Or a door that you can close to signal to everyone that you are, indeed, working.

Personalization. You need a work spot that allows you to put your personal stamp firmly on it. When you look at your space — that corner of your family room or that guest room you just converted — it has to give you comfort and be right for you. It must be a place where you can accomplish your best work.

Setting Boundaries

Your business is the newest member of your family, and you — and your family members — will need to treat it as such. That means you need to help your family understand when you are in your mother and wife roles, and when you are being the business owner. Setting these boundaries usually includes talks about three things: Time, Space, and Need.

Your whole family needs clear definitions of when you have set your work hours, and everyone — including you — should try to keep these consistent. Of course, nothing is written in stone, but if you can carve out some very specific times and even post them up on the fridge or your home office door as a reminder, this helps everyone at least understand when you're trying to get work done.

You also need to clearly show everyone in your family your specific workspace and differentiate it from the baby or kid space or the whole family space. Walk them through your new office so they understand where you will be when you are working. Draw distinct lines so you can avoid confusion and keep peace in your household. We don't mean you have to literally draw lines on the floor to make it clear where you're working, but then again . . .

"Setting boundaries was crucial for us," says Lisa Lehmann, the owner of Studio Jewel. Within three months of starting, she knew she had a viable business. And a viable business needed space to exist and expand.

"Since this was going to be my full-time vocation, and I was not willing to sacrifice being an at-home mom, we knew it was imperative that we purchase a home with dedicated space for my business."

Entering into that "boundaries conversation" with her entire family was an important step for Lisa. "This was a big commitment," she explains. "My family needed to understand Mommy was not working just because she wanted to be busy; Mommy needs to and wants to work."

And that required real workspace, especially for a labor-intensive business like Lisa's. So the Lehmanns moved into a home that provided Lisa with the arena to allow her creative juices to run free. In her studio, she has the space to design and handcraft her individual works of art, take orders, and fulfill her customers' needs. And when she closes the door at night, she's done.

For Shafonne Myers — as for many of us — moving into a new home wasn't a realistic option, but she was determined to have the perfect in-home-office solution that allowed her to work and keep an eye on her young son. The family decided to turn their family room into a space that is part playroom, with about one-quarter of it dedicated to Shafonne's office for her event-planning business, Making Your Event Special.

"It works well for us because since my son is only one, it allows me to let him play, but I'm still right there. He is a bit clingy since I've been at home with him, so it allows me to work, but he still can see me and feels I'm still there." She continues, "And also, since it's downstairs, he is free to walk around the downstairs without me worrying."

Since this arrangement allows Shafonne to feel peaceful while she works and takes care of her family, she doesn't imagine making any changes or graduating to a different office setup anytime soon.

CHEAT SHEET: How to Hold the Conversation about Work and Your Workspace with Your Family

1. **Family first.** Your family needs to know they come first in this equation. Make sure you remind them, "You are the most important people in my life."

2. **Show mutual respect.** You respect family time and require that your family respects your work time. "Together, we can make this work."

3. **Make promises you can keep.** If you say you're going to stop working at 5:00 p.m. and won't start again until the kiddos are in bed, do that. If you need to work on Saturdays but make a commitment to not work on Monday nights during softball practice, keep your word. "I promise not to bring my phone to the table during meals. That's my commitment to you — to give you my full attention during those times." Say it. Mean it. Do it.

4. **Manage expectations.** Make it clear what you can and cannot do and when you cannot do it. "Mommy can't play with you until after lunch time. Enjoy your lunch, and when you're done, we can play for a little while."

5. **Ask for input.** You can't unilaterally set all the rules in this new situation. What does your partner need? What do your kids need? You're pretty much at the mercy of what your baby needs, but we'll tackle childcare in Chapter 6. "What's important to you? When do you need me to be available?"

6. **Look for happy compromises.** Not every compromise will make everyone happy, but as you give in a little and your family gives in a little, you can find workable solutions, so in the end you create a way to run a business in your home. "I'm willing to stop work at 5:00 p.m. if you can do your homework as soon as you get home, so we can all have dinner together."

Yes, we did it, too. We had the talk with our families.

Aliza's experience

I find separating work and home life very challenging. I have had long discussions with my husband about how my business is a company and is a real job, and that just because I work from home doesn't mean I'm not working. We've also discussed my need for at least six hours of uninterrupted time during each weekday to get work done. I'm lucky if I get four, but this isn't his fault — he's at his job doing his work.

I'm living in an area in rural Alaska where childcare is scarce. Sometimes, I may get a few weeks of six- to eight-hour workdays during the school year, while my daughter is at school in the morning and then goes to a babysitter's home in the afternoons. Then — too often to count — a babysitter isn't available, and my daughter ends up home with me midday. Summers can be tougher as there are no organized activities for young children in our community. In the past, I'd shuttle my daughter between playdates and babysitters, or she'd be home with me while I tried to work.

It can be hard to tell a five-year-old that she cannot interrupt Mommy when there is no one else in the house but us. She can only keep herself busy on her own for so long, but she really does try. I get creative and designate various activity times for her, such as art time, book time, movie time, doll time, blocks time, and even iPad time (mine is chock-full of educational kids' games). And yes, outdoor time, which is so great for her but usually impossible in the winter, when it is consistently colder than -45 degrees. In the summertime, I try to join her outside, if only for a few minutes sitting on the front porch in the sun while she plays in her sandbox. The fresh air and sunshine always do me good, even though I'm hard pressed to ever leave my computer.

If the week has been a wash due to too many interruptions, my husband knows that on at least one of the weekend days he is on Daddy Duty to watch the little one so I can catch up on work. I think the fact that I'm running a business isn't always real to him until I deposit money at the beginning of each month into our joint bank account, but he is getting better over time in terms of understanding that I don't only want to work but *need* to work.

Danielle's experience

As my business has evolved, I have recognized the juggle to be both mom and business owner is perpetually a work in progress. Initially, I was a traditional "stay-at-home" mom. My one and only focus was my family. But I started to get the itch. When I first realized there was an additional calling for me, I dabbled in other people's businesses. I planned weddings. I could fit the "at-home" portion of my job seamlessly into my schedule, since the work didn't require much time. And when the client's wedding day arrived, I would leave the house to do the work.

But once I started my own business, I found it challenging to explain to everyone around me — my husband, my children, even my friends — just what I was doing with my time. Starting a business takes hardcore elbow grease, and in the beginning, you often have very little to show for it. So I asked for trust. I looked my husband in the eye and told him my overall goal: to contribute financially to our family with a viable business by the time our youngest, Cooper was in school fulltime, and to eventually have enough of an income to provide him the freedom to choose a career path he truly enjoys. Then, I asked him to trust two things: 1) that while my path, my schedule, even my work itself might seem unconventional, I did know what I was doing; and 2) that I would reach my business goals.

He agreed. And so far, from both of our perspectives, that trust was well placed. I have achieved one of those goals, as I do, in fact, have a viable business that allows me to contribute financially to our family. And I did it ahead of schedule. I have not yet reached the point that I can support our entire family as ho has, but I'm working on it.

My conversations with my kids still happen daily. I think my biggest job is to manage expectations. For six years, I didn't miss anything. I was present for first words, first steps, and every school event, as well as soccer and T-ball games. I recognize that it is hard for my children to understand that I can't be around for every single moment anymore. I have shared with them how important it is to me that they respect my desire to work. However, I never let them forget that I understand how it can be tough for them. And that it is often tough for me as well. It is a give and take. There are days I feel we have it all under control, and others when I'm hanging on for dear life.

But this is part of the journey.

I hired someone to clean out the extra room to make a comfortable office space. Simply too big a task with a toddler running about!

—Sara Bobkoff, Native Content & Communications

Create Your Home Office

Carving out a workspace can be harder in smaller quarters. Regardless of space issues, there are ways to make an office in your home feel like a legitimate workspace, and by proxy, make you feel like a business owner.

Here are some quick tips to get the most out of a smaller space.

CHEAT SHEET: Space-Saving Tips for Creating a Productive Workspace

1. **Go vertical.** Consider a multitiered computer desk that could house your computer, printer, and/or fax all in one spot. A bookcase or shelves could also store many of the business books and items you use on a regular basis.

2. **Consider a multipurpose filing cabinet.** A cabinet on wheels can be moved easily from one area to another, can store many of your files, and can also provide an additional flat working surface if you need one to spread out your work materials.

3. **Get organized.** Take advantage of the multiple organizational tools on the market to manage the clutter on your desk space, instead of stacking paper and peppering office supplies all over your work area. Think bins, holders, trays, and boxes.

4. **Convert a closet.** With a little construction and some creativity, you can put a desk or table in a closet, build in some shelves, roll in a filing cabinet, and voilà! Not only do you have a workspace, but it's one that you can hide at a moment's notice when company arrives.

If you have the luxury of space, such as an entire room for your office, watch out for clutter creep. Sometimes, it is far easier to keep a tiny space tidy than it is a whole room. And sometimes you need to bring someone else in to help you clear the clutter away. See Aliza's story about hiring a personal organizer in Chapter 6.

How creative can you get with your workspace? Well, Heather Solos, owner of Home-Ec101. com and author of *Home-Ec 101: Skills for Everyday Living — Cook It, Clean It, Fix It, Wash It,* spent a number of months working in her master bedroom closet until she finally took over a portion of her kids' playroom, since they're at school during the day. Laura White-Ritchie, owner of Brainyfeet.com and LauraGetsGraphic.com, is mom to two older kids, 17 and 21, and four-year-old twins, so her house can get busy and noisy. She uses the family camper adjacent to her house as her home office. Talk about creative!

The Well-Equipped Workplace

Beyond making space, having the right tools and equipment at your disposal is important for productivity. It is great if you have a desk, but without a computer and Internet connection, you might face a few challenges.

In Chapter 2, we recommended a half-dozen business ideas, all pretty low cost to start and powered by the Web, so a computer in those cases is essential. Even the moms with online stores selling nontechie products, such as jewelry and hair accessories, still rely heavily on their computer and Internet access.

Let's go into a little more detail about the essentials for your home office.

Your first needs are likely business-specific equipment, such as a sewing machine for making accessories, jewelry tools and beads for customized creations, or paint and clay for arts and crafts.

Cristiana Rodrigues of Carpe Digi digital consulting, and mom to a two-year-old son, says she can't work without her iPhone and iPad. Stephanie Campbell of Campbell Communications says her most important piece of equipment in her home office is . . . her cappuccino machine!

HANDY CHECKLIST: 10 Things You'll Need to Maximize Productivity

○ **A Work Station.** This can be a desk or table, along with a comfortable, preferably ergonomic, chair. Ergonomic is a design that fits the human body and lets you sit and work with the least amount of wear, tear, and stress on your back, shoulders, neck, and arms — body parts that are always affected by poor posture and regular office chairs. Make sure your work station is big enough to have space, but not so big that it becomes a storage area.

○ **Computer.** No surprise, right? You can get a desktop computer for a screaming deal or go for the portability of a laptop, a smart choice if you're in a tight space. Do your research to figure out what type of computer might fit your business best. For example, if you work with video like Danielle, a MacBook or MacBook Pro might be your best choice, and it comes with iMovie already installed, a fairly easy-to-use video-editing software. And while you're buying, upgrading, or equipping your computer, don't forget about the software. Microsoft Office is pretty much a staple for any home office, but you may need specialized software for your particular type of business. A lot of software these days can be accessed on the Internet, including documents (for example, Google Docs); project and task management programs (Basecamp, 5pm, and Wrike); accounting (Freshbooks, QuickBooks Online); and so much more.

○ **Internet/E-mail.** Again, no surprise here. Access to the Internet gives you the ability to do research, connect to others, and engage clients and customers for your new business. The Internet can also be an invaluable platform for branding yourself and marketing your company. See Chapter 7 for more about branding online and leveraging technology. E-mail, of course, has become a main method of communication in business. Regardless of what e-mail software or system you use, you want to be able to access your messages from anywhere so you can connect as needed when you aren't at home.

○ **4-in-1 Printer.** With the low prices of printers these days, there is no reason you should go without a 4-in-1, even though, as we pointed out in Chapter 2, many Web-based businesses do very little printing, faxing, scanning, or copying. At the very least, you will want the ability to print basic documents and contracts and to scan them after you sign them to e-mail them out. If you prefer, you can use sites like Echosign and Docusign, which allow you to easily sign contracts electronically that are secure and legally binding. What will they think of next? If budget is an issue, get the most features in a machine that you can afford and what you can't buy now, plan for later, if you need it. And don't forget, many a home-business owner often takes regular trips to the local copy shop.

○ **Phone.** Though the online world and technology are extremely valuable, there will still be times when your clients or customers need to reach you for setting appointments, brainstorming, checking on orders, you name it. Even if you handle most communications via the Internet, a phone can help keep you personally connected to the people you are serving. When you have little face-to-face time, speaking by phone can be the next best thing. We're also big users of Skype for free long-distance calls over the Internet.

○ **File Cabinet, Folders, and/or Storage Space.** Having a place to store all your office files and documents is key to staying organized. You might have paperwork coming out of your ears, but if you have a distinct place to file that paper, no sweat, right? No matter what type of business you decide to start, there will inevitably be proposals, contracts, orders, and reports that need to be filed in a suitable out-of-the-way place with easy access, so you are able to find whatever you need whenever you need it.

○ **Recycling Box or Trash.** You are going to produce trash, and in order to keep your office space under control, you'll need to have a receptacle nearby to dispose of items you no longer need. If you have recycling in your area, make sure you separate as you toss things out so you're not struggling with that later. You will also want to consider a paper shredder for disposing of sensitive documents.

○ **Bulletin Board/Whiteboard/Memo Pad.** Another organizational tool to keep you on track is some kind of board to post more pressing items and information, such as a corkboard, an oversized calendar, a chalkboard, or a whiteboard — anything that helps you keep track of deadlines, important dates, upcoming projects, and those ubiquitous Post-it Notes.

○ **Basic Office Supplies.** There are a number of things that can be handy for any home office, but if you're on a budget, start with only the things you are certain you'll need. Among the essentials are: pens, pencils, notepads, binders, reams of copy and printing paper, binder clips, paper clips, a pair of scissors, a Scotch tape dispenser (with rolls of tape), a stapler, a hole puncher, and a labeler. Even a letter opener can be a helpful thing to have around.

○ **All-About-You Items.** Whether it's your favorite coffee mug, a family photo, a quote, an award, a splash of color, or something else that inspires you, you need to put some personal touches in your home office. Danielle displays a classic photo-booth-style photo of her family. Aliza has an aromatherapy infuser with an uplifting blend of eucalyptus, ginger, and cardamom (from Aromandina).

I've always worked from home creating jewelry by hand, so my children don't know any different, they are used to it, but when they were young, my space was completely off limits because it was dangerous. They knew if mom had a torch in her hand — don't come in.

—Lisa Lehmann, Studio Jewel

Danielle's workspace

I have an actual office in our home with a desk, bookshelves, and a slew of personal effects including this quote: "Happiness is never something you get from other people. The happiness you feel is in direct proportion to the love you give." — Oprah Winfrey.

But the initial challenge I faced was that my small people were too small for me to feel comfortable being hidden away from them — even in the most amazing of spaces. Also, this office is one I share with my husband, which is fantastic . . . when he's not here. When he is here, he actually has to work, too, and that requires him to be on the phone. That isn't conducive to the quiet I need to write or edit. So over the past few years, I've found myself increasingly on the couch, in the kitchen, or packing up to head out the door to Panera.

My mistake? Early on, I didn't stop to think about what kind of space I needed to maximize my personal productivity. I thought: OFFICE = GOOD, so my husband and I created one. Later, I realized it wasn't fitting with my workload and family responsibilities, but when I tried to manage both in the kitchen, I found that I only gave half of my attention to each. That didn't work either. Coming full circle, I now know I need an office to keep myself in line, and I know that an organized space is a happy one. Having an area that is solely dedicated to work allows me to have the separation I need desperately. I can now give the appropriate attention to my business dealings when I'm working, and when I'm off I can focus entirely on my family rather than dividing my attention.

Aliza's workspace

I, too, have an actual office, but one-fourth of it has my husband's dresser and closet, because our master bedroom is too small to fit them. The rest of the room is mine. I have a desk, four filing cabinets, and several low shelves around the perimeter of the room.

And I have piles. While I preach organizing, filing, and keeping down clutter, I'm a bit of a hoarder (something I'm definitely working on) and tend to cluster little piles all over the place. One good thing about the space is that it does have a big window and gets some light, but a downside is it can also be chilly; I often turn up the heat, which then makes me a little sleepy.

Even with a door that I can close to signal to my husband and daughter that I'm working, there are inevitably many knocks on it during the day or a little head poking in and a tiny voice asking, "What are you doing, Mom?" Hey, it comes with the territory. I sometimes vary my workspace by carrying my laptop to the dining room or the living room, but I try to leave the laptop back in the office and close the door at the end of the day so I don't compulsively check my e-mails.

Out-of-Home Spaces

Have you ever had one of those days where you feel as though you just live at your office? Oh, that's right — you do. If you are working from home, those two words, "office" and "home," may have become interchangeable. You might be working until you drop into bed, waking the next morning to grab your coffee, still clad in your pajamas, and wandering the 15 feet to your workspace, wiping sticky fingerprints from your computer screen as you begin yet another day "at the office."

You know that time you yelled at your children to KINDLY KEEP IT DOWN while you were on hold on the phone, waiting for a client to pick up? Only you weren't on hold after all. That may have been the moment you realized you needed to tackle some work in a space where a screaming toddler wouldn't be a distraction. There will be times you need to work out of the home, specifically for clients or just for your own sanity.

"I used to lie in bed at night and hear a fax coming in late and feel compelled to see what it was," says Kat Gordon, owner of Maternal Instinct, about the time she had a home office. "Or I would have a conference call in my office with the door shut tight and my toddler son scratching at the door like a lovesick puppy, no matter how my nanny tried to engage him in play "

For Kat, the biggest challenge of starting a home-based business had an easy solution: don't have it at home. She ended up getting an office just for herself outside her home, and she has the flexibility to come and go as she pleases. Kat's office is just seven minutes from her home and is small – 170 square feet — with lots of light and an open-air courtyard in the center. She decorated it in a fun and feminine style, she says, because she lives in a house of males.

Kat's office space costs her $450 per month, plus she has to carry insurance on it, and that adds about another $100 per month. Then there are the costs for phone, Internet, etc., which are about another $100 per month.

Says Kat, "I cover these costs via my work for clients. It's a necessary expense and tax write-off. Plus, I often host meetings here with clients."

Having an office outside the home doesn't mean she doesn't sometimes work from home, such as when one of her sons is home sick from school or she needs to let the repairman in.

"Every once in a while I'll work from home just because I get in a groove working on something at home and won't want to break the spell by driving elsewhere," says Kat.

The biggest benefit of all, Kat says, is that when she walks in the door at home at the end of the day, she's "Mom." Nothing else. She disconnects from her laptop and spends time with her kids. So where can you go to maximize productivity, but without a huge hit to your bank account? We're not suggesting that you get a full-time office outside of the home, especially not at the early stages of your business. After all, the whole point of this book is to start a home-based business. However, we also didn't want to neglect mentioning that option.

Certainly, the luxury of working in your bunny slippers — not to mention all the free coffee a girl could want — might be tough to find elsewhere. But in the name of business — *your business* — you may want to consider out-of-the-home work options, on either an as-needed basis or on a semiregular basis, for a change of pace. For some people, and you may be one of them, being out of a cubicle or a structured office environment unleashes creativity and increases productivity. For others, you'll need to get used to working from home versus an office, and that's okay.

Local Cafés and Coffee Shops

It is hard not to be a fan of friendly neighborhood cafés or coffee shops with free Wi-Fi. Danielle is partial to Panera, a national restaurant chain that has yummy lunches and speedy Wi-Fi. Spending the cumulative total of weeks working in one of their booths and being on a first-name basis with most of the employees, it can feel as though you've hung up a temporary shingle on that booth right there by the window. When in the city, Aliza likes to frequent small, locally owned cafés and coffee shops for their eclectic, homey environments as well as tasty food and Wi-Fi connections, but in her rural Alaska community, the options are down to one restaurant (there are two in her area, but one allows smoking and doesn't have Wi-Fi, so that isn't an option for her).

The benefits of working at your local café or coffee shop are clear:

- Free Wi-Fi.
- A temporary space of your very own (that you don't have to clean up).
- A distinct lack of children and toddlers clamoring for your attention. They might be there, but they aren't yours to handle.
- A place for you to focus (as long as you can stand the low roar of chatter).

The downsides? You have to lug your work with you. The volume around you comes in waves, increasing around lunchtime, so you may want to schedule client calls during the "down" or quiet times of the day. The Wi-Fi could be slower than what you need or on a timer to limit you to an hour. You could feel the compulsion to purchase coffee and a bagel every time you enter, which hits both the budget and the waistline. If that is the case, your "café-office" can feel pricey by the end of a week. Only you can assess if you walk out of the coffee shop feeling like you've gotten work done, or if you're just jittery from too much coffee and stimulation. But if you do find cafés and coffee shops to be the right respite from day-in and day-out working from home, just don't forget to budget for a generous tip to the waitstaff!

Considering Coworking

A coworking space takes the café or outside-the-home environment to the next level by providing a more structured office setup that you share with others. You can collaborate with individuals in the space or work independently. In many cities around the world, formal and informal coworking spaces are forming, and a quick Google search will present dozens of options. There's even a "casual work event" that happens all around the world called a "Jelly," where people set up impromptu shared workspaces in someone's home, a restaurant or café, or even an actual office. You can learn more about these unique events at WorkAtJelly.com.

More formal coworking spaces offer multiple desks or work stations, where you can work for days on end and pay a "membership" fee of sorts to the owners of the space or the group that is organizing it, for longer-term needs. If you only want or need an office space for a few days, some spaces let you "pay as you go." Other coworking arrangements are entirely free.

One example is St. Louis Coworking, which is contained within a 10,000 square-foot space in a building in downtown St. Louis. They have 48 dedicated desk/work stations and more than 30 additional stations for "drop in" use, and are open from 9:00 a.m. to 9:00 p.m. during the week and 9:00 a.m. to 3:00 p.m. on Saturdays. Their desks are filled with people from a variety of professions: independent workers, entrepreneurs, Web designers, graphic designers, creatives, musicians, artists, bloggers, attorneys, CPAs, architects, real estate agents, salespeople, and more.

A solo dedicated desk costs $450 per month and includes a custom U-shaped desk, a chair, and a filing cabinet intended for the use of one person. A shared dedicated desk is $300 per month. A monthly "drop in" fee of $100 provides access to any designated open work areas, Wi-Fi, power, and, of course, coffee. For those who prefer to swing by on a daily basis, they can expect to pay $15 each time they do.

Workers can also use the St. Louis Coworking address to look official and businesslike by going for the Virtual Office package for $175 per month, which includes mail collection, forwarding/call-answering services, and drop-in member privileges. As a result of the creative nature of a coworking environment, there will be chatter in the building, but most facilities have enough space to allow people to spread out.

In addition to the member benefits of Wi-Fi or hardwired Internet, power, free faxes, unlimited coffee, light printing, a business address, and conference room hours, there may be other perks, such as lunchtime workouts and pancake breakfasts.

"I couldn't stand working at home all alone. I would get completely distracted and think about the laundry or what I am cooking for dinner. I would start cleaning up," says Jill Stern of nail polish strips company, Nail Fraud. "I guess I am a major procrastinator."

Jill heard about a shared workspace and resource for women business owners called In Good Company in New York City and jumped at the chance to join. She has had an office there for three years.

Says Jill, "They keep it very clean and nice-looking in there, which makes me feel good. I have nothing on my desk so my thoughts can't wander. And I have met other like-minded businesswomen and I often sit in on their workshops and learn from others."

If you would like a dedicated out-of-the-home office space without the open, "coworking" atmosphere, you can look into an "office share," which allows you to sublease space in someone else's office. The advantage to this is that you can find an environment that fits your business and work style, be it formal or extremely casual. Want to bring your dog to work? Find a space that will allow it.

As you can imagine, with the changes in the economy, many companies have downsized and are looking for ways to utilize their empty workspace. This is an especially useful option if you need to conduct a lot of in-person client meetings or work in the same space as your contractors. Renting space in an actual office setting means you don't have to meet everyone over coffee at the local Starbucks again and again.

Your office share will likely be furnished, and you have the option to sublease anything from a single desk to a number of office spaces. More often than not, this sharing will provide you access to business conference rooms, kitchen areas, and other common spaces. In most cases, you will also have the use of Wi-Fi or hardwired Internet, telephone, and fax, and you may be able to negotiate the shared use of a receptionist.

And finally, you can probably sign a short-term lease, so you aren't locked into any situation for too long. Prices usually range from about a hundred dollars to over a thousand per month, so shop around, because you'll most likely want the smaller, less costly option. These solutions are usually found in major cities such as San Francisco and New York City, but some smaller communities may also set them up to help generate revenues off of unused workspace. Resources like ShareYourOffice.com and LiquidSpaces.com (which has a mobile app to find open, affordable drop-in workspaces) are great places to start your search for the perfect office share.

Why YES, I Am Working. Thank You for Asking!

The burden every work-at-home mom must bear is that there will be people who don't believe you are actually working, because — *really*? Gasp! — you are at *home*. We've all heard the jokes, seen the eye rolls. We've smiled through the snarky remarks about Oprah and how nice it must be to sit around eating bonbons, and have bitten our tongues when someone asks, "How's that little Web site of yours doing?"

We know you want to yell, "That little Web site is supplementing my family's income, paying for our summer vacation, buying our new car . . . " But — and this is a big but — your energy is better focused in other areas, like your family and that "little Web site." (wink)

You can help the people around you to take you and your business more seriously by treating it as a serious endeavor yourself. Part of doing this means mastering the art of saying "no" to things that take you away from work when you should be working. Keep in mind that if you left your house each morning to drive to an office, you would not be available to babysit your friends' kids, you would not be available to be the emergency contact on a snow day for "working parents," and you would not be available to drive your neighbor to the airport.

The same holds true for you now. You are a woman with a business. You have work hours. Sure, you have flexibility, but when someone asks you for a favor because you're home, let him or her know that you would love to help out, but you are working.

Say it with us. "No, sorry, I can't. I'm working at that time."

Feels good, doesn't it?

Now that you have mastered the many aspects of your workspace, we bet you are wondering how you are going to juggle all of this — your children, your home, and your business — *all by yourself*. Well, the short answer is: You aren't. You don't need to do it alone. You are going to need help. Read on to find out the "who," the "why," and the "how much" for getting the help you need in your new home office.

Moms Know Best

Respect your time so others will do the same.

—Dionne L. Stalling, Journeys in Travel, LLC

Chapter 6
Bringing in the Reinforcements

How is your cape fitting?

You know, the one with the great big "S" for "Superwoman" on it? Is it feeling a bit snug? We thought it might be, and we're here to tell you: It really is okay to take it off. In fact, that one little step — not trying to do it all totally by yourself — will do you a world of good.

Know Your Limits

You can't do everything — create the business plan, set up the company books, make the product or offer the service, tackle the marketing, build the Web site — all while juggling a baby on the way, little ones, school schedules, volunteer activities, cleaning your home, running the PTA, and having a hot meal on the table at the end of the day. You may be an overachiever, but you aren't invincible, right? You might be a little (a lot) crazy trying to do it all.

We assume you are smart enough to surround yourself with people who are more skilled than you in some of these areas or who have the time — and often their own business — to help you take care of some of these responsibilities. If you've been waffling on outsourcing to other people, this chapter will hopefully nudge you in the right direction. We'll explain how you can afford to hire others to do things for you, and we'll cover such creative ideas as bartering and understanding your worth. For example, if you have a Web design business, you could build a Web site for your bookkeeper in exchange for a few months of bookkeeping services. For others, you'll have to pay, but we'll help you determine whom to pay and when to pay them to actually save — or help yourself make — money.

Giving up any portion of control of your life and work is likely one of the most difficult things you will ever do. Many of us think what we "do ourselves" is a measure of our self-worth. Some of us think that we're the only ones who know how to do what needs to be done or that we're the only people in the world who can do it right. Somewhere along the way, we became convinced that doing it all ourselves meant we were saving money and that asking for help was a sign of weakness.

This is a myth. A MYTH, we say.

Asking for help and hiring contractors who have a certain level of expertise that we don't posses — or the time and inclination to do the things that we shouldn't be spending time on — makes us more intelligent and, in the long run, gives us a far greater earning potential.

> *The key to maintaining my sanity? I have learned to ask for help when I need it. I have assistants who help manage my day-to-day tasks with my company, as well as an extra pair of hands at home. My "mother's helper" takes some of the household chores off my shoulders. It has helped me to have more time to sit and focus on my family instead of fussing at them for not helping me do chores.*
>
> —Alli Worthington, BlissDom Events

Help with Baby

When you have a newborn, it may be easy for you to accomplish tasks during your little one's extended (and multiple) nap times. Or it might be a really hard thing because you're supposed to be napping when the baby naps, and we encourage you to put your health — and sanity — first. As your little ones grow older, their needs will demand more of your attention, but often at different times of the day. No matter what stage you're at in terms of mommyhood, you need time to dedicate to your home and family, and there is only so much time in the day. You may find you need to call in the reinforcements in order to accomplish the same amount of work you used to be able to do, pre-kids.

One smart thing any mom with a home-based business can do is to hire a part-time sitter or nanny to come over to the house a few days a week or a few hours a day. This will give you some breathing room and actual uninterrupted time to focus. This is a good thing.

Hiring a part-time sitter or nanny — or even turning to family if they are nearby - isn't just good for business. Realize that the "free hours" you have to work when someone helps you with your children (or around the house) allow you to be fully present when you are with your family, because you got some actual work done. If you are splitting your time and energy, responding to e-mails as you make dinner, taking calls while giving your child a bath, or using the television as a babysitter, you not only hurt your productivity but you start feeling guilty about your inability to dedicate love and attention to your family. You may think you are saving time and money, but you are actually increasing the amount of time it takes to accomplish each task. Remember, in business, time is money.

Amee Quiriconi says she couldn't have made her business, Squak Mountain Stone, work without outside help.

"From day one I had my mother-in-law help me. I selected my first shop outside of my garage because it was near my in-laws' home. She was invaluable, especially when I had my second child while in the early days of my business."

Have we convinced you that in-home childcare is a great option? We sure hope so! Depending on your budget and your needs, you can bring in a full-time nanny or hire a local teen as a mother's helper for just a few hours a week and notice a huge return on your investment in no time.

So, where do you find the right person to bring into your home?

Services like Sittercity.com, NannyLocaters.com, and Care.com can help you with the search to find a skilled and screened childcare provider. This is a step you can take even if you are expecting. It doesn't hurt to have done your research ahead of time. According to Nanny Locaters, as of 2010, the average cost of a nanny living outside your home was $500 to $700 for a 45- to 50-hour workweek. A nanny who resides in your home earns between $400 to $600 for the same hours, since you are also providing her with room and board. Part-time babysitter rates run the gamut, but every community has a range that is acceptable pay for babysitting, usually from $5 to $15 an hour. Look for childcare providers who have taken CPR and First Aid; someone who has those important skills takes babysitting seriously enough to invest their own time and money in gaining knowledge that can save lives.

Another option is home-based childcare. You can check with your local or state government for listings to find suitable, licensed childcare providers located in someone's home. If you find a home-based provider, check with the family services agency that oversees childcare businesses to make sure you're dealing with providers who are reputable and have an environment that's safe and clean. A solution outside your home does require that you round up the little ones and bring them to another location, but you'll return to a very quiet, work-conducive home office. Big sigh. Home-based childcare providers range in price but can be less than $500 per month, or at least less than daycare centers.

One daycare center that has a national presence is called Childtime Learning Centers, started and funded by Gerber, the baby food and products company. Fees range from $150 to $300 per week, depending on the age of your child (more expensive for younger and non-potty-trained ones). They offer a range of services from infant daycare to afterschool programs for children up to 12 years old.

Danielle on childcare

Childcare has been a moving target for me over the years, but the one thing I have always known is that having someone help with my children while I am working makes me a better mother when I am not working, freeing me up to focus entirely on them. I'm lucky to have loving in-laws close by who adore spending time with my small people, as well as a neighborhood full of responsible babysitters.

With two young children who love their mommy and are used to a lot of attention, it was a challenge to attempt to work and give them the love they deserve. Trying to explain to small people why I have to work or how I just need "one more minute" is not only challenging but guilt inducing in a way I found hard to stomach. I definitely worked my tail off during nap times and after they had gone to bed, but found that I was more peaceful knowing someone was taking good care of them during the few daytime hours that I chose to work. I was a more productive business owner and a more fully engaged mommy when I was with them.

Aliza on childcare

Not to be a broken record, but I live in a rural community with very little resources for young children and a revolving door of babysitters. When I was still in a city, I used craigslist to find qualified babysitters that I carefully screened before hiring. I knew they'd be coming to my home, and I'd be in the next room, so I was never nervous about leaving my baby with a "stranger."

In the last few years since we moved to a rural area, we've had almost a dozen different sitters, most of whom did not babysit at our place but wanted me to bring my daughter to them. The first several moved away. Some went back to school or off to college. Some took other non-babysitting jobs. It is a constant challenge trying to find consistent childcare, even for a little girl who everyone says is a joy to watch.

But I'm a firm believer in having someone help me with my daughter. She's a smart, inquisitive child and very social, so she thrives on a lot of attention. She loves to talk. And talk and talk. Knowing that when I have work, I have a hard time with being interrupted, hiring someone else to watch my little one gives her the social interaction she craves and provides me with the quiet time I need to complete my projects.

When I don't have time to work, I get frustrated and sometimes even angry, and that's not healthy for anyone — not me and not my family. I see paying a childcare provider as an investment in both my business and my mental health. Paying someone else to provide childcare is totally worth it because I feel much more guilty snapping at others for interrupting me than having someone else share childcare duties with me.

Learning to say "no" is key. Yes, we have had sitters for a while. I just cannot do any software development in 15-minute chunks, so it was a very conscious decision. Finding shared office space has also been really good for me. And I do have a "no-device" policy when I am with my kids. As a result, I tweet a lot less but am learning to live with it.

—Maya Bisineer, founder, Memetales

Help Around the House

Let's see: mother, wife, homemaker, business owner. Something's got to give.

Julie Aigner-Clark, creator of Baby Einstein and producer of *The Safe Side* child safety videos, found it very difficult to hire somebody to help around the house in the early days of her first business.

"It was weird for me to hire somebody to do things that I thought were my job," she admits. "I was doing all those things: laundry and cooking dinner, and I was working, and I was being a mom. I looked at those three things and thought, 'Which one don't I want to do?' Definitely laundry."

Julie says that hiring someone to help around the house back then not only freed up more time so she could work on her business, but it also allowed her to be with her small children.

Here are some ideas for getting the help you need so you can get more done:

Housekeeping. If you find yourself constantly putting off vacuuming until "tomorrow," forgetting to take the laundry out of the dryer, or writing your name in the dust on your bookshelves, it may be time to hire someone to tackle the heavy-duty cleaning — even biweekly. You can find someone to do household chores through Web-based classifieds, national maid services like Merry Maids, or even just asking your friends or women in your neighborhood.

Cooking. Mealtime can be an important time for families, but trying to have a healthy, hot meal at the ready after your day-long juggle can be daunting. Luckily, there are services out there for putting nutritious meals on your dinner table. Depending on your budget, you can try an "assemble yourself" meal-prep solution from such national chains as Dinners Ready, Make or Take Gourmet, or Mr. Food. These services allow you to purchase ready-to-go dinners or to put together a number of dishes in advance at their storefronts to save you time later. Meal-prep companies give you peace of mind, knowing you are feeding your family well-balanced meals without having to dedicate hours to cooking every day. Or you might try a local meals provider who puts the meals together for you, or even a personal chef. Both options can be surprisingly affordable, such as $15 to $20 per entrée. If you're using this service for only a few meals a night, the expense may be worth the reduced stress as mealtime is nearing.

Gardening/Landscaping. You might be one of those people who feels gardening is an escape, a mind cleanser that helps you to decompress and refocus. But you might also find that mowing the lawn or trimming the rose bushes is a task you detest because it is taking more time away from the two things you are enjoying the most — your family and your new business. Whether you hire a neighborhood teen, an independent gardener, or a landscaping company to tend to your lawn and plants, look at it as money well spent, because you'll be in your home office making more money.

Errands. Grocery shopping, picking up the dry cleaning, waiting for a repairman, personal shopping: these just might be the things that consume most of your time. Did you know there are companies that offer these services, so you can hire people to do these tasks for you? Look for personal assistants, personal concierge services, and errand-running businesses, although concierge services can sometimes be on the pricier side. You can find these helpful companies by doing a Google search or checking your Yellow Pages or other local business directory. Since they usually provide in-person services, few offer these services nationally. However, a new company called TaskRabbit is looking to expand beyond San Francisco and Boston and may be available across the country by the time you read this.

Janelle Miller owns two businesses: a cleaning and restoration business, Integrity Cleaning and Restoration, and J and J Inspirations, where she creates custom aprons, dresses, art smocks, and other attire. For her, hiring a grocery delivery service was the key to sanity.

"Have you ever shopped with a teen, a toddler, and a newborn? Between the two businesses and three boys, cutting out duties, such as grocery shopping, is such a blessing. Our local grocer offers delivery to us out in the country for $9.00 per delivery. This is such a minimal fee for all that I am saving!"

The bonus? Janelle says she has extra time to snuggle with her little ones or work on her businesses.

Bartering for Help

Wonder how you're going to afford to pay for all this great help? Why not barter? Bartering is an equitable trade of services that replaces or supplements monetary payments. Many businesses are open to bartering because every business owner has particular needs that will cost them money to fulfill.

Need someone to run errands for you? Perhaps you've found someone just starting her personal concierge business; you can offer to market her business by building her a page on Facebook — because that's one of your skills — and based on both of your prices, that is a fair and equitable trade. Voilà! You've both gotten something done without having to fork over cash. Keep in mind that bartering still takes time, and time is money — you know the drill.

Leah Warson, maker of handmade, scented beanbag-like sachets through her company, Whiffy Bean Bags, found bartering to be extremely useful.

Says Leah, "I've traded quite often. I would trade my product for handmade clothes, handmade hair bows, Web site work, handmade soaps, product pictures, and fabric. I was always more than willing to barter; it was a lot of fun and totally beneficial to both sides."

Laura White-Ritchie of BrainyFeet made a trade when getting her business off the ground. "I made a Web site and a logo for a friend who did two years of taxes for me. Totally worth it!"

Virtual Assistants

There are people out there ready to help take a load off you if you let them. They take on the busy administrative work or small office tasks to free you up for the bigger stuff. This is a service you may want to secure before your business overwhelms you. So, expectant moms, this is the time to do the research to find the right person for you.

"If you are spending time on things you could pass off, that is money you could be out making," says Kelly Morrison, owner of The Virtual Peacock, a virtual assistance company. "From a financial perspective, you pay yourself a lot more to do administrative work than you would a virtual assistant. This means you are potentially losing money every time you tackle these items on your own."

A virtual assistant (or VA) is a professional who provides administrative, creative, or technical support to another professional, both usually working from their own "home offices" and often entirely online, meaning they never meet face-to-face; hence the term "virtual." We talked about starting a virtual assistance business in Chapter 2 because of the low entry cost and the flexibility it gives you. Now let's look at virtual assistants from the other side — to help you!

Kelly Morrison is in her third year as a virtual assistant and owns her own business, The Virtual Peacock. She assists small business owners with their day-to-day marketing and customer service, and all the work is done via phone, fax, and e-mail.

"Some people are initially hesitant to pass off work, but the longer they work with a virtual assistant, the more willing they are to do it," Kelly explains, adding that once trust is built, handing off tasks becomes easier.

Virtual assistants can tackle such time-demanding tasks as answering e-mails, writing press releases, scheduling appointments, managing your social media, and creating online content for your business. Because you are letting a VA into your inner circle, it is important to make sure you are hiring the right person.

According to Kelly, there are a few things you should keep in mind as you interview people for this position:

1. **Do you like their communication style?** If you don't interact well with them initially, expect subsequent conversations to be strained, making it difficult for you to work well together.
2. **Make a list of everything you do in a week's time.** Share that with your potential assistant. She should be able to tell you which items she could take

off your plate. This will help you to understand the individual's skill set, as well as how much time you will be gaining by hiring her.

3. **Find someone who is interested in your brand or business.** You want someone who actually *cares* about the product or services you are providing. This will make her more invested in the work she does for you.

4. **Ask for references.** It is comforting to hear from another client how the assistant works, and asking for references is good business practice.

Some virtual assistants work on a retainer, which means you are guaranteeing them a certain number of hours to work each week. With a retainer, you usually pay in advance for those work hours, and then they work down the retainer. Other VAs are willing to be paid on an as-needed basis and at an hourly rate. You need to estimate how many hours your tasks might take, or go by your budget to determine what you are willing and able to pay. In some cases, you can make an offer based on what works for you, as some VAs are flexible in terms of how they work with clients. Other VAs have fixed prices or packages; for example, you can purchase a package of five hours for $150, or a package of ten hours for $275, a little discount for guaranteeing them more hours of work.

To find a VA that might work for you, Kelly recommends Assistu.com, a free registry that allows you to specify how many hours you might need someone, the qualifications you are looking for, and even what time zone you would prefer, to make it easier to communicate in a timely manner. She also suggests vanetworking.com and ivaa.org for finding VAs who have been specifically trained to set up their own businesses, manage their work-from-home time, and offer assistance to clients. Some virtual assistance agencies include TodaysAdmin.com and LongerDays.com.

Nicole Johnson of BabySleepSite.com swears by her virtual assistant:

"Being a mom means that there is always something that needs to be done, so I work really long hours, including late nights. I have not overcome it quite yet, but having a fantastic VA has helped me a lot with productivity."

Nicole doesn't think her business would be where it is today without this kind of help, and says that although hiring a VA initially decreased profits, her business has grown far faster than she could have done alone:

"Believing that paying for help is worth it was hard for me, but if I could do it again, I'd do it sooner!"

CHEAT SHEET: How to Work with Your Virtual Assistant

1. **Decide your communication preferences.** What works best for you? E-mail, phone, even text messaging? And how often do you want to communicate with your VA? Once a week or once a day or as often as needed?

2. **Choose the tools you want to use.** Depending on what you need help with, your VA may be able to take hours of work off your plate. But you need to know how to work together. For example, will the work take place in your e-mail account or an e-newsletter service or blog publishing tool? If they help you keep track of tasks, what system will you use? Producteev, Cohuman, Remember The Milk, or a simple shared document in Google Docs are just some of the handy collaboration tools you can use with your VA. If they are managing your schedule, do you use Google Calendars or some other calendaring system to which you can give them access?

3. **Set a schedule.** Will they be working for you every day or just every Monday? Budgeting for some scheduled work time but also some "I need help right now" time helps cover both predictable and unplanned needs.

4. **Set deadlines.** You both need to be aware of the expectations for each project and when you need them done. Do you expect work to be completed in 24 hours or by the end of the week? Be clear about deadlines so neither of you is frustrated or disappointed.

5. **Allow a grace period for you and your VA to get to know each other.** No working relationship gels overnight. It will take some time for you to let go of some of the reins and delegate, and it will take time for your new VA to get a feel for your work style.

As with any expenditure you have in business, you need to make sure you can afford to pay for this, but you also need to consider what would happen if you didn't pay for it. This is sometimes known as "opportunity costs," where you miss an opportunity to close a business deal or complete a project and get paid because you didn't think you could "afford" to hire help. Whenever you spend money on your business, make sure it helps you achieve your short-term and your long-term goals.

Tapping into a Crowd

There is another way to get busywork done, particularly small and repetitive tasks that don't take a high level of skills but need to be done. You can "crowdsource" your tasks, a variation of outsourcing where you access a large number of workers who perform small tasks — called "microtasks" — to get something done. Tasks you can crowdsource include double-checking contact information, verifying phone numbers and addresses, cleaning up a database of information, identifying objects in images, labeling or renaming images, adding tags or keywords to images, and the list goes on and on.

If you have hundreds or thousands of tiny tasks that need to be done, you can use Web sites such as Mechanical Turk, Crowdflower, CrowdCloud, and Clickworker to handle your projects. Need audio transcribed? Try Castingwords. Need a name for your company or product? Try NamingForce. Need some beta testing for your Web site? Try SquadHelp or uTest. To learn more about crowdsourcing, you can read how businesses are using it on sites like The Daily Crowdsource and Crowdsourcing.org, or stop by MomIncorporated.com for lots of crowdsourcing resources. We also mention "crowdfunding" — another aspect of crowdsourcing — in Chapter 4.

If you are looking for some design work but your budget is more in the range of a couple of hundred dollars versus a thousand or more, you can submit a creative brief to a design competition site such as 99Designs, Crowdspring, or Prova. On those sites, designers read your creative brief where you explain what you need — logo, business cards, fliers, online ad banners, Web site design — and your preferences such as colors, styles, and samples of other designs you like. Artists choose to respond by coming up with a design and uploading it to the crowdsourcing site for your review. You can end up with dozens of possible designs, and you can request a few revisions to get you closer to what you want. When you choose the one you like, the winning designer gets paid, usually between $50 and $500, depending on the site and the job.

Aliza turned to crowdsourcing for a fun logo for her company Mediaegg. She chose the crowdsourcing site Prova, and posted a creative brief that explained that her favorite color was pink, and she liked it in combination with brown. She also said she wanted a play on the word Mediaegg, but not a symbol or icon. She received nearly 50 designs in response to her query, and she quickly zeroed in on a few designs that appealed to her.

She asked a few of the artists for revisions, then directed her friends and colleagues to the design competition to vote on their favorites. In the end, she picked the logo that was the third choice of her network, a cute robotic-looking egg in pink and brown, an entirely unexpected choice for her. In total, she spent a handful of hours reviewing designs and about $250 for the design she picked.

As you can see, there are many creative and innovative ways to get things done as you set up and run your business. Knowing when to turn to others for help is practically a skill. Our advice? Always do it sooner than you think you're going to need it!

I might have fun tinkering, but it is not the best use of my time. I set financial goals for myself because this reminds me that I must do the tasks that are most profitable. If I want to make "X" amount of dollars, I know that paying someone with expertise gets me to my end goal.

—Gina Axelson, Bella Forma Pilates & ThePilatesBiz.com

Danielle on delegating

I've learned a lot since starting my business. It is amazing how much time, energy, and money I could have saved along the way if I had only known then what I know now. Writing this book has filled me with knowledge that I didn't have before. Take, for example, the quote above from Gina Axelson about "I might have fun tinkering, but it is not the best use of my time." Somewhere deep in my soul I knew this to be true.

I could spend my days making list after list of all the things that need to be done, but I am, in fact:

a) unable to do them because who *really has enough time, anyway?*

b) not accomplishing many of the "to-dos" because something else always takes precedence.

c) only focusing on the short term — the tasks that are paying me right now instead of taking care of the items that will benefit me in the long run.

But then I am in a perpetual state of stress and am not growing my business properly. The day after I interviewed Gina for this book, the stars aligned, and I hired a virtual assistant. For nearly four years into my journey as a business owner, until I started working on this book, I repeatedly forced myself back into the "you-can-do-it-yourself" frame of mind. My in-box, my To Do list, and my business in general have suffered as I kept reaching a maximum capacity that stunted my ability to grow.

The truth is, *I can't* do it all, and I shouldn't do it all because much of what I need done — accounting, legal issues, promotion — falls outside my comfort zone. And I don't have the time, the energy, or the desire to learn to wear an additional 25 different hats. If I would like people to hire me for the skill set I bring to the table, doesn't it make sense for me to do the same — to reach out to people who can do it better and make my life a million times easier?

The one exception to my lack of delegation has been the designing of my Web sites. I have been asking for help in this arena for quite some time. I will freely admit that HTML is a language I do not speak, so I have relied heavily on the considerable talent of Sierra Friend, The Blog Site Coach, to guide me and to create the sites I currently run. There was a time when I actually considered taking classes in HTML — something that in reality does NOT interest me at all. Fortunately, that was a fleeting thought, quashed mainly by my inability to fit the classes into my already packed schedule. And for that, I am grateful. I've learned that it is best to leave jobs I do not understand and do not want to the people who do.

Aliza on delegating

I have always had a hard time delegating. For many years, I was guilty of the "only I can do it the right way" school of thought. But over the years, I've learned hard lessons from trying to do everything myself. If you work with smart and talented people, you won't be disappointed with the work they do. If things don't meet your expectations, it is often because you didn't explain things well in the first place. So I've worked hard on being better at explaining my needs.

One of the best things I ever did for my home office was to hire a personal organizer. She went through boxes and boxes of old bills, reports, proposals, contracts, and random paperwork, and came up with a logical and easy system for reorganizing everything. How anyone could stand doing that kind of tedious busywork was beyond me, but this woman loved her work and excelled at making sense of chaos. That reminds me that I'm long overdue for another organizational overhaul, and I know it will be worth every penny.

More recently, I've been working with several virtual assistants. Each time I think I can't afford one or try to work with one who charges smaller fees, I realize that you get what you pay for, and have learned that an excellent virtual assistant is worth the higher fee because he or she works faster, more accurately, and knows how to take work off your plate with very little instruction. I have to admit I still sometimes have a hard time defining what I need at any given moment, but a really good virtual assistant knows what questions to ask to pull out of you exactly what you need. What a relief!

We hope this chapter has given you some ideas to get the help you need. Even doing a search on Google or asking your family, friends, or colleagues for ideas and referrals can be other good sources for support.

Ask for help. It is a big thing to recognize when you need help, and an even bigger leap to ask for it or to hire someone to provide it. Recognizing your strengths and how your business is best served by leveraging other people's strengths are two of the things that make you a *smart* business owner.

So, go ahead, take that leap. Hire some help. We promise, it will be okay, and you'll be able to fly without your cape!

Write down a list of everything in your business that has to be done, and then put a star by the things that can ONLY be done by you. Spend time each day figuring out how you can delegate everything else so that you are working from your gifted zone and doing what you really love.

—Sarah Cook, Raising CEO Kids

Chapter 7
Lights, Camera, Action . . .
Starring Your Start-up

Build Your Brand

Building your brand? This is about you, your business, and the people you want to reach with your business. Who are you and what do you stand for? Who is your target market? This is your opportunity to prove not only that you have skills, but that you have the ability needed to do the job you want to do. In branding, this is referred to as "delivering on your brand promise."

Dan Schwabel, the author of *Me 2.0: Build a Powerful Brand to Achieve Career Success*, points out in his book that "your personal brand is, first and foremost, about the person. The clearer you are about your destination, the easier it will be to communicate why others should pay attention."

We can learn a lot about branding from top brands. Take a look at some of the biggies. Nike is one of the premiere examples of a strong, memorable, and enduring brand: Just do it. You hear the name Nike. You picture the swoosh — a great example of a powerful logo. You hear the slogan in your head. You know what they stand for and how they expect you to act. You buy into the message and the brand promise with your purchasing power. Sure, you're buying high-quality sportswear and gear, right? You'll probably be able to perform better with their shoes or workout clothes, right? These may be things we believe somewhere in our minds because we trust the brand Nike to deliver.

Best Buy is an example of a brand name that "says it all." You immediately understand that this is a company that believes they are providing the best product for your dollar. They also offer their strongly branded Geek Squad — the men and women who will take care of all of your technical needs. They have taken the "geek" factor way over the top with the pocket protectors, the too-short pants, and the short-sleeve button-down shirts. Their geeks also drive around in bright, Geek Squad–branded Volkswagen Beetles. You can't help but find their geekiness just a little chic. You can't help but remember them the next time your computer is on the fritz or you need a new digital camera.

Then there is Yahoo! and Google. From the time you first heard these companies' names, you could already imagine the creativity and energy inherent in the work they do. While their names aren't descriptive, they probably made you curious and willing to find out more about them, even before you understood just what they were doing. Their names attracted you and maybe even made you smile. What a great thing for good brand names to do!

All of these companies have spent millions of dollars to infuse their brand names with meaning and feeling. They've also had to back up their brand promises with quality goods and services. Their brand names are all known for something.

What do you do that people should know? Why should others pay attention to you? Back in Chapter 1, we encouraged you to think about what you're good at as well as what you're passionate about, in order to determine the type of business you should start. In a sense, your business is an extension of yourself, and what makes you and your business stand out is, in part, your brand.

Your brand is the beginning of a conversation. Who is talking about you, and what are they saying? If they aren't talking about you, how can you get them to do so in positive ways? What expertise do you have to share with others as part of this conversation to establish your brand? What do you want people to know about you and your business? These are all questions you need to be asking yourself as you work at establishing and promoting your brand.

Danielle's brand

I didn't set out to create a "brand," but I now realize that everything I do — with both ExtraordinaryMommy and DanielleSmithMedia — is infused with my own beliefs and personality. The ExtraordinaryMommy "brand" is positive, upbeat, and inclusive — I always wanted the site to be a place that was welcoming to all moms, so I rarely, if ever, venture into politics, religion, or anything controversial. I have never wanted anyone to feel excluded. My goal has always been to make EVERY mom feel extraordinary.

Additionally, I believe one of my primary responsibilities as a person — and therefore as a parent — is to be a good citizen of the world. I must do that by living it, by modeling it, not simply by talking about it. Every day on Twitter I ask, "Who has good news to share?" Part of my brand — in the case of both ExtraordinaryMommy and now DanielleSmithMedia — is taking that "good" and spreading it. I want to maintain the "give good, get good" mindset that was in place when I started this journey. This doesn't mean I don't have bad days. It simply means that I choose to keep most of those bad days to myself.

The DanielleSmithMedia brand is all about how social and media intersect — it is a combination of my background as a television anchor and reporter (a love of media, information, and reporting), my current love of all things video, and the present state of the "social" aspect of social media.

When thinking about your brand, it helps to ask yourself what you want people to think about when they walk away from an experience with you — and this can be in person, over the phone, or virtually. For me, I hope my desire to share "good," coupled with being kind, honest, and inspiring on some level, is prevalent. My passion is video and includes storytelling, interviewing people, and doing correspondent work, and I hope people think of these things when they think of me.

Aliza's brand

When people ask me who's my idol, I always say Madonna, because of the way she took charge of her career and continues to reinvent herself to stay relevant throughout the years. So, for me, reinventing my brand is part of how I stay current in my industry, because technology changes so quickly. After starting the first woman-owned Internet company called Cybergrrl, Inc., I have been known for my work to empower women through technology.

As the years change and my business focus changes, knowing who I am and what I do can sometimes get jumbled. I've had to think long and hard about my brand lately, and I realize that what I do really well includes creating content that empowers and inspires. I'm passionate about exploring and learning new things and then sharing that information in a way that is easy to understand.

I developed a new brand: She Knows Social. I love teaching, guiding, and explaining things, and that's what I'll do with the She Knows Social brand. I love helping others find their own "aha" moments, whether by defining a technology term for them or by telling stories that help them see new ways of doing things in their professional or personal lives. I hope that when people consider my brand, they think, "Helpful, honest, generous, inspiring." Those are really important qualities to me, and they inform everything I do in business and in life.

WORKSHEET: Brand-Building Questions

Once you know the answer to these questions, it will be easier to determine your brand-building path, both off- and online. You can download a copy of this questionnaire on MomIncorporated.com.

Who are you, and what do you do that your audience should know?

Why should others pay attention to you?

Who do you want to reach, and *where* are they located?

Where are they gathering, exchanging information, having conversations?

Who is talking about you, and what are they saying?

Who *might* be talking about you, and if they aren't, how can you get them to in positive ways?

What expertise do you have to share with others as part of this conversation to establish your brand?

What else do you want people to know about you and your business?

Using Technology to Build Your Brand

If you're working from home, you need to leverage all the Web has to offer to run your business smoothly, establish your brand, get your name out there, and build a positive reputation. There are so many places where technology plays a critical role in any company, from the tools you use for your day-to-day work to the ways you communicate and promote what you do. Let's start with the fundamentals of creating your Web presence — your Web site — and then talk about social media marketing for brand-building.

Landing Your Domain Name

Having a Web site is certainly an important tool for any business, but even more crucial is having your own domain name that reflects your company brand. A domain name is the main part of a Web address that people type in to find your Web site, such as Mediaegg.com, AlizaSherman.com, DanielleSmithMedia.com, and ExtraordinaryMommy.com. No matter where you host your Web site, you can reserve a domain name and arrange for it to lead to your site.

An easy way to look for and reserve a domain name is to use a registrar, which is a company with the authority to reserve, distribute, and manage domain names. A popular registrar is GoDaddy.com, where you can enter in variations of your company name, along with different file extensions such as .com, .net, .biz, .info, .us, and .tv. Finding a .com may be tough, so you may have to choose a different extension. When you search for YourCompanyName.com in GoDaddy, you'll know immediately in the search results if it is available, and you'll also be given a list of other available extensions.

Remember that your domain name should reflect your company brand name or trademark as closely as possible (see Chapter 3 for more information about trademarks). If your company name is ABCDesigns but you cannot get ABCDesigns.com, you could try ABCDesigns.biz or ABCDesignsLLC.com

Domain names can range in price from $5 per year to $35 or more per year, depending on how coveted the name might be. Also, the .tv extension tends to be pricier than other extensions.

Using Your Domain Name

Once you have your domain, there are two things you'll want to do with it right off the bat. The first is to make sure it points to your Web site. Depending on how and where your Web site is being developed, you could either give your Web developer instructions to host your domain name on the same server where your site is being hosted, or you can easily point it to any other Web site address.

On GoDaddy, for example, you simply select "Web Forwarding" on your domain name and type in the exact address where your site's home page is located. The way you point your domain name to your Web site can affect how easily your Web site can be found in search engines. Search Engine Optimization (or SEO) is an online marketing technique you can use to "optimize" your site in order to gain a higher ranking on popular search engines. A higher ranking means your site shows up as close to the top of the first page of search engine results as possible when people search for words related to you, your site, or your products. The theory with SEO is: the higher you show up on a search results page, the more visitors you will have to your site.

The other way you want to immediately use your domain name is for your business e-mail. You'll look a lot more professional if your e-mail address is Jane@JaneCompany.com than if it were Jane@hotmail.com, although this perception varies depending on your business, industry, and even location.

A quick, easy way to get your custom e-mail address is as you are registering your domain name. Most registrars will also offer branded e-mail, so when you reserve YourCompany. com, you can sign up for e-mail hosting as well.

Another free way to not only get e-mail using your own domain name, but also other useful online tools for your basic company communications needs, is to sign up for Google Apps. The search engine company Google also offers many Web-based applications, and bundles some of their applications for business owners. Some of the handy software includes:

- Custom-branded e-mail.
- Calendar with mobile access.
- Live instant messaging — text, audio, and video.
- Shared documents, including word processing, spreadsheets, presentations, drawings, and forms (compatible with Microsoft Office files).
- Google Sites to create Web pages easily for internal or external use.

The free Google Apps account includes up to 50 custom user accounts, so it can be just the right package for a solo-person, home-based business. Some other options for online suites of business apps include Zoho (free and paid versions) and Feng Office (about $10 per month).

Getting a Web Site

There are so many options for Web sites these days that we're going to focus on viable free and inexpensive options. Most companies simply need a professional-looking presence online rather than a high-end, robust, database-driven site. Once you pick your Web site publishing solution, you can point your new domain name to it — or arrange to have your domain hosted along with your now Web site.

Here are a few things to ask yourself to find the best publishing and hosting solutions for your site:

1. What kind of site are you mainly seeking?
   a. Basic, with company background and service offerings.
   b. Something more interactive, with a blog.
   c. A place where I can display and sell my products.
2. What is your preferred budget?
   a. Free to under $100.
   b. $100 to $600.
   c. In the $600 to $1,200 range.
3. How often do you think you'll need to update it?
   a. Hardly ever.
   b. About once a week.
   c. Anytime I need to do it.

If you answered with mostly a's, you may want to try these options:

Register.com, NetSol.com, or GoDaddy.com. These are three of the most popular domain name registrars that will offer you easy-to-use templates to build a site with low-cost hosting. Keep in mind, you'll have limited design flexibility, and not all templates look great. But if you're on a budget and can't afford a designer, this may be a good way to launch a basic site.

Wordpress.com. This is a site that offers hosted blog publishing software that is very easy to use. You can select a free theme or pay a small fee for a designer template, and then set up your site so you have a static home page instead of the blog format.

If you answered with mostly b's, you could use the following options:

Wordpress.com with a Purchased Theme. You could pay $50 or more for a designed theme or template that can take your site to the next level. You could also pay a few hundred dollars for a Wordpress designer to help you customize your site a little bit more.

Virb or SquareSpace. Both of these sites have affordable rates for high-impact and elegantly designed templates with site hosting (Virb is $10 per month or $100 per year; SquareSpace is $144 to $432 per year).

If you answered with mostly c's, you could try the following:

Wordpress Hosted. If you want more control and flexibility over your site design, you could move up to a hosted version of Wordpress and add many more features and a more customized theme or template, usually created with the help of a Wordpress designer. The more complex your design, the more you'll pay a designer, and it could run you into the thousands — so be aware of costs up front, so you're not hit with a big bill later.

Etsy. If you have a product, you might want to start selling it through a site that walks you through all the steps of setting up an online store. Etsy is a popular option, particularly because of its powerful community of creators and buyers. There are fees involved to setting up your shop, but this is still an affordable option. Some people also have success with eBay or smaller marketplaces such as Zibbet, ArtFire, and Folksy.

Melissa Mullinax has a store called Spun Candy on Etsy. As a seller of products online, she says her experience with Etsy has been wonderful.

"Even setting up a shop was fairly painless," says Melissa. "Everything is nicely laid out step-by-step. Just be aware of the little fees for listing items — they do add up if you're not careful."

Erin Elwood of Erin Kate Create is also a fan of Etsy.

"The clean design of the Web site lets the images of the products shine on their own — no bright, busy backgrounds distracting from the site's real focus of the handmade items for sale," says Erin. "Many artisans and crafters — myself included — aren't Web aficionados, so Etsy's user-friendly options for creating, managing, and sharing storefronts on other sites are a big attraction."

Erin adds that when she has clients who aren't local, she loves being able to share product images, and get payment and receive shipping information, all in one common place through Etsy.

Danielle's site

When I truly started to take this entrepreneurial endeavor seriously, I opted for Wordpress Hosted. I use a StudioPress Theme that was modified by designer Sierra Friend. Hiring Sierra to create my Web sites was one of the best decisions I have made. The work she did in a matter of days would have taken me years to learn. If people find your site difficult to navigate or not pleasing to the eye, they will instantly click away.

When I first jumped online, I had an actual site created from scratch — I'm certain you can just picture me up, late at night, eyes crossed as I stare at page after page of HTML code — it may as well have been written in Czech. In addition to the actual site, I had a separate blog on Wordpress.com. Streamlining the two with Wordpress Hosted was a smart move. With the way my site is set up now, not only can I make adjustments easily, but the clean format allows visitors to jump simply from one page to the next.

Aliza's site

I've opted for Wordpress Hosted as well. I've been using a free theme, which is what Wordpress calls their templates, but I've also added some customization with the help of a consultant. I've toyed with the idea of purchasing a theme but haven't gotten around to it yet (maybe by the time this book comes out, I'll have done it). I'm also a little kooky in that I have about ten more sites and blogs that I publish.

My very first blogs were started on Blogger, which is a good place to start a blog. Then I moved them to Typepad; three of them are still there, but the rest are on Wordpress.com, the free hosting and publishing site. I find the Wordpress features to be easy to use, plus the software itself is so popular. I can always find people who can help me when I can't figure something out.

There isn't one single right way to get a Web site developed and hosted. You could work with an independent Web designer and choose an independent hosting solution. But if you're on a tighter budget, there are ways you can do it yourself and then bring in a professional on an as-needed basis.

Social media makes us relevant. It normalizes the playing field. We are competing against publicly traded companies who have a direct relationship with the consumer, and we have a base of followers just like the big boys.

—Selena Cuffe, founder, Heritage Link Brands

Building Your Brand with Social Media

Facebook, Twitter, LinkedIn, oh my! Social media is a set of online tools that help you communicate, build community, and share information. These tools have changed the way we make friends, nurture our networks, establish our reputations, build our brands, and conduct business deals all around the globe. Social media can come in the form of social networks like Facebook and Twitter, video-sharing sites like YouTube and Vimeo, photo-sharing sites like Flickr and Instagram, and so much more.

Social media is how we are sharing the news of our businesses and telling the world what we love and what we don't. We are "friending," sharing, promoting, and marketing using social media tools. But more important, we have the individual power to publish our own words and bring together our friends, fans, followers, and customers to create our own communities, to have conversations with them, and build relationships.

The first thing you need to know about social networks is that you don't have to be on every single one you find. Pick the one or several that you want to be on, based on a few key things:

1. Who you're trying to reach. Where do they gather and communicate?
2. What you're trying to do. Are you selling and promoting product, or are you trying to establish your credibility and showcase your expertise?
3. What you're comfortable doing. Do you like publishing new articles every week, or do you prefer asking a question and starting a conversation?

Some tools are better than others for reaching the right people and encouraging the right actions. More than anything, you have to know your personality as well as your resources — including how much time you have available — before you start dabbling in marketing using social media tools.

Here's a quick quiz to determine which social network is best suited for your needs.

MOM QUIZ: What Social Network Suits You?

We're going to focus on Facebook, Twitter, and LinkedIn for this quiz because they are the three most popular social networks. After taking the quiz, you should have a better understanding of which one of these networks will work for you or which one you should focus most of your efforts on.

1. How much time do you have?
   a. No time, no time at all, and the thought of making time makes me crazy.
   b. I know social media marketing is important, so I'll try to carve out some time, but not much.
   c. I understand that social media marketing can help me be more efficient with brand building, so I'll definitely incorporate it into my schedule.

2. Who are you trying to reach?
   a. Businesspeople, busy professionals, my industry peers.
   b. General consumers, people interested in conversations and community.
   c. People who are savvy about tech and who seek quality information online.

3. What do you want people to do?
   a. Hire me or refer me to others.
   b. Buy my products or hire me.
   c. Hire me, do business with me.

4. What do you like doing most?
   a. Network in a business setting.
   b. Host a gathering.
   c. Give advice and share information.

5. What do you hate doing?
   a. Making small talk.
   b. Being more formal and businesslike.
   c. Writing lengthy messages.

Now let's see what top social network is right up your alley . . .

If you answered with mostly a's, then you may want to look at LinkedIn. LinkedIn is a professionally focused social network where you can create a profile based on your resume and business accomplishments. Your best use of LinkedIn happens when you connect with your actual contacts, and you can easily use LinkedIn for referrals to others through the site's networking tools.

Carla Young, founder of *MOMeo Magazine* and cofounder of Entrepreneurial Moms International, uses LinkedIn to seek out strategic connections.

"Where Facebook and Twitter are more social, LinkedIn is more serious and business focused," says Carla, who also uses LinkedIn to send out news releases and information blasts.

"Unlike Twitter and Facebook, where it's gone within a blip, those announcements and promotions stay put within the post category on LinkedIn."

If you answered with mostly b's, then you probably already love Facebook. Facebook is a very sociable place where real-life and new friends connect and where consumers can connect with companies. People who use Facebook love to be part of a community and take the time to have real conversations. The tools and applications offered on Facebook can help you create a truly interactive and multimedia presence with images, video, polls, forms, and so much more. Never underestimate the power of friendly connections on Facebook.

"Facebook tends to be just a place my friends and family keep up with how I am doing in business rather than getting hired. Although one high school friend had me do her Web site, and she has connected me to several clients," says Mariah Sinclair Humphries of Jula Studios.

If you answered with mostly c's, then you might really like Twitter. Twitter is great for rapid-fire information exchange. Your messages are limited to 140 characters, and that really forces you to get to the heart of your message. You can certainly hold conversations on Twitter and build and be a part of a community, but the flow of Twitter talk is more like a rushing river, whereas Facebook is like a calm pool where people gather.

"The network of supportive people I found on Twitter encouraged me to start blogging," says Jen Taylor of Mocha Creative Works. "I did, which led to getting articles published and creating my company. That led me to joining EverythingMom as their community manager and working freelance for a writing company."

With our social network quiz, we're not telling you to only be on one social network, although we would advise you to start with one, get very familiar with it, and build a strong following. If you're already on two or three of them — and even some others — do an assessment to make sure that each one really helps you achieve your business and brand-building goals.

Once you have determined whether your social media network of choice is Facebook, Twitter, or LinkedIn, it is best to arm yourself with some clear information on how to get started, rather than just diving in and getting yourself nervous about the things you might not know. Go to MomIncorporated.com for our handy tips for using Facebook, Twitter, and LinkedIn. Now let's hear from some more moms on social media.

Facebook Faves

Mom entrepreneur Jodie Valenti recalls the genesis of her company on Facebook:

"With a tight, tight, tight budget and a newborn at home, I decided to make a fancy cake for my son's third birthday," she says. "I had never baked and had no formal decorating experience, but over the next few months I made a few cakes for family and friends, all the while posting them on Facebook to show them off."

Jodie posted a cake that she made for a friend's birthday, and by the end of that day, seven people messaged her to ask if she was taking orders.

"I said sure, and Cakes, Cupcakes & Cookies . . . OH MY! was born," says Jodie.

Carla Young refers to social media as "a communication tool and a listening tool." She has had success using all three of the big ones — Twitter, Facebook, and LinkedIn — but finds different levels of success with each, based on what she's trying to do.

She explains how Facebook works for her companies: "Pages and Groups allow us to connect and communicate with our Facebook fan base, but more important, it builds community within our fan base. We see a lot of member-to-member communication on Facebook because we consider our pages an open venue for them."

One of the tactics Carla uses on Facebook is tagging, which is a feature that allows you to create links when you mention another person on Facebook who you know or a company's page that you've liked. Another tactic she uses is posting questions through Facebook Questions, an interactive feature where you can ask your Facebook friends a question to get their attention, get answers, and start a conversation.

She also creates what she calls "Theme Days" on her Facebook Pages. For example, Tuesdays are "Tag It Tuesday," where fans of her companies' Facebook Pages can tag her companies by name, and she tags each one who does in return.

Says Carla, "This is a cross-promotional trick that boosts visibility for both of us."

Johanna Parker of Kaya's Kloset says Facebook has been an amazing tool for promoting her company as well.

"I love seeing pictures of people's children in their baby shoes and slippers! I use my Facebook Page to announce shows, new fabrics, and contests — and the personal interactions with my customers have been wonderful. As busy moms, we don't always have the time to read the e-mails that come through our inbox, but a short update from a favorite shop . . . I always have the time for that!"

Twitter Treats

We love Twitter as a communications tool for our businesses, and we're not alone. Amanda Duke of Cutie Pa Tutus says she couldn't live without Twitter. "Twitter is probably responsible for about 70 percent of my wholesale and retail sales; its power is not to be discounted."

Originally, Amanda thought Twitter would be a waste of time, but she allowed a friend to talk her into signing on about six months after starting her business. In what turned out to be a brilliant marketing move, Amanda sent actress Denise Richards a "Cutie Care Package" and asked her to tweet if she liked the tutus.

Richards did. And the Cutie Pa Tutus Twitter account skyrocketed from 80 followers to hundreds overnight. Her Twitter account also caught the eye of quite a few retailers — including one in Russia and one in South Africa. Suddenly, Cutie Pa Tutus was international!

Now, Amanda makes tweeting a regular part of her marketing:

"I tweet about raising my kids, pop culture, and then, of course, the company and new products. I purposely try to keep my ratio of woman/mom to work-based tweets at about 60/40 or sometimes even 70/30, so followers can get to know us on a personal basis. I find that my business attracts more customers — and more loyal customers — in my target audience when they identify with me personally on some level."

All of this from an original marketing budget of about $25.

Danielle on Twitter

I can trace everything I currently do back to my initial dive into Twitter. The ability to connect with people in both personal and professional environments has been invaluable. It was actually an encounter on Twitter that led to my covering the 2010 Vancouver Winter Olympics for P&G as a correspondent.

In the late summer of 2009, I was chatting on Twitter with Stephanie Smirnov, the President of DeVries PR. I was delighted to meet her in person for the first time at a conference later that year. As we talked, Stephanie decided I might be a fit for a project her firm was working on at the 140 Conference, at the Kodak Theater in Los Angeles. I was brought in to do interviews and cover the event as a video correspondent. Since that project went well, my name came up to work in the same capacity — but this time for P&G (a DeVries client) at the Winter Olympic Games. If Stephanie and I had not connected first on Twitter, our meeting at the conference might not have had the same impact.

Aliza on Twitter

Without a doubt, Twitter is my favorite social media tool. Since joining Twitter in early 2007, I have been able to maintain a high profile amongst both my industry peers and my audience, usually from my home in rural Alaska. I've had people tell me, "I've seen you everywhere!" I'm not everywhere, of course. But I'm on Twitter daily.

For me, checking Twitter starts my workday, even before checking e-mails. I then check into Twitter periodically every few hours during my day to get answers to questions, to see how I can help others who are asking questions, to promote something I'm doing, to see what's happening in my industry and in the world, and sometimes just to express myself in a forum where I know somebody is listening. Twitter helps me feel less isolated when I'm far away from family, friends, and colleagues.

LinkedIn Love

LinkedIn is far more business oriented than Facebook and Twitter, and for some people it is an acquired taste. For example, Aliza uses it specifically to reach out to business owners and professionals for her more "serious" projects, posting to it about once a week, and only more frequently if she is promoting something to a work-related crowd. Danielle, on the other hand, receives the greatest engagement via Twitter, YouTube, and Facebook. Since these are the venues where she primarily devotes her time and energy, she only uses LinkedIn to maintain a professional presence and to showcase her resume. Other women are much more devoted to LinkedIn and find it indispensible for their businesses.

Robin Gorman Newman, founder of Motherhood Later . . . Than Sooner, finds LinkedIn to be a valuable business tool.

"LinkedIn is one way I keep on the pulse professionally without attending tons of networking functions and conferences. My schedule doesn't always permit me to get out as much as I'd like," says Robin.

Using LinkedIn, Robin has reconnected with people she knew in her pre-motherhood days as a public relations pro in New York City. She also uses her LinkedIn profile to showcase her skills to obtain consulting work.

Says Robin, "I've joined LinkedIn groups, and have connected with companies to explore advertising opportunities for my site, MotherhoodLater.com. Plus, I've networked through LinkedIn with potential promotional partners to create alliances, and use it to obtain content from authors, experts, and mom-owned companies to publish on my site."

Regardless of which social network or networks you're using to build your brand, consider the 80/20 Rule: 80 percent of what you say or share should be conversation or other content you think people will find useful, and 20 percent should be promotional. And *always* be honest. If you're tweeting under your own name but are representing your company, make that clear. If you make an offer on your Facebook Page, always follow through. Whatever you add to your LinkedIn profile for credibility, make sure what you say is true. Good news travels fast online, but bad news travels faster. Don't get into a brand disaster by being dishonest, inappropriate, or inconsiderate.

On MomIncorporated.com, you can also find our "Dos and Don'ts List for Using Social Media." Check it out!

Getting the Right Clients and Customers

If you're starting a service business, the people buying your services are usually referred to as clients. When you're selling products, your buyers are your customers. To keep things easy, we'll call anyone who buys from you "customers." Regardless of the terminology you use, no matter what business you're in, customers are your lifeblood. But they can also be your downfall if you aren't strategic about whom you target to purchase your products and services, and aren't prepared to serve them.

Depending on the type of business you start, you need to clearly establish what you will be offering your customers. You've probably thought about your customers to some extent in the business planning section of Chapter 3, where we asked you to outline what benefits you're providing them. Remember this?

What need are you solving for your customer? Emphasize benefits!

When thinking of customers, you don't only need to think about what you offer them — you also need to think about who they are and what they might ask from you, above and beyond what you offer. What do they want and, more important, how will you prepare to handle their demands?

If you have a service company, your clients may demand more of your immediate time and attention than if you sell products online, but a products company may face more refund requests. If you sell online, you usually get paid immediately and before you deliver products, but if you are providing services, you most likely get paid after services are rendered or through a payment plan, so the risk of receiving money late is very real. If you are selling products online through a secure and reliable e-commerce system, you'll be able to verify payments, and therefore will receive full payment for products before they are shipped. Providing services may also mean you are at your clients' beck and call far more frequently. How can you minimize excessive demand on your time and attention when running a business?

If you're giving out your phone number on your Web site, you might want to consider a free voicemail system like Google Voice. This system will ring any phone you'd like, but if you don't pick up, it takes both a voice message and translates it into a text message that you can opt to receive via mobile phone. Make sure you set parameters and express what you consider acceptable calling hours on your Web site.

How customer intensive is your business? The right customers can make all the difference in the world, especially given your "home with baby" work environment. Starting a service company out of your home with little ones around, you already have a specific situation that might require a specific type of client. You should interview your clients just as extensively as they interview you, keeping in mind their work style, expectations, and even their tolerance for a baby crying in the background or for family emergencies that might come up.

While you may not always have a choice, depending on your type of business or the industry you're in, chances are you'll have a much less stressful workday if you have clients who understand your work situation.

Take it from us: We know that no matter how well you set up your work environment, you have to expect the unexpected just about every day. Be up-front about your work situation — if you can — to both gauge a potential client's tolerance and to prepare them. Only you can tell whether or not it is a good idea to broach the topic of screaming babies, but if you cannot, then you have to work extra hard to create the most conducive work environment for professional dealings by phone. Make sure your phone has a mute button. The mute button will save you from embarrassment more times than you can imagine!

Aliza's ideal client

I'm lucky to work predominantly on projects that are female focused, and most of my clients are either women with children of their own or men who are fathers, some of whom also work from home. I'm always up-front with my clients when my daughter is home sick or when we're without a babysitter. Almost inevitably, my best attempts to keep her occupied fail about 20 minutes into a client call. I use the mute button heavily, or use emphatic hand gestures to visually ask my daughter to please wait, please be quiet, to Please. Stop. Talking. But be forewarned: gesticulating wildly while on the phone usually just increases your child's desire to chatter more and more loudly.

What I might lack in a fully quiet and professional work environment, I make up for by striving to produce high-quality work, delivering it promptly, and taking really good care of my clients. In this day and age, as more people start home-based businesses or telecommute, the perils and pitfalls of working from the home are things many of us share. I find more and more clients to work with who totally get the work-from-home dynamic, so that means less explanation is needed on my part, and that's a big relief.

Danielle's ideal client

I have yet to work with anyone who hasn't been respectful of my "work-from-home" status. I'm extremely lucky to have partnered with individuals and brands that appreciate me as both an entrepreneur and as a mother, so my working relationships have been fluid. I'm always honest with clients about my schedule, and they are honest about their expectations for the work we do together. Like Aliza, I've waved wildly, made angry faces, and even mimed stomping my foot while my small people interrupt me on the phone. And more often than not, they pretend they have no idea why I'm turning red in the face.

When we run our business from home, our schedules are fluid, and the hours we keep are often unconventional. I've been known to work until 2:00 or 3:00 a.m. We do prioritize both family and business, and enjoy the benefits of working in a nonstructured environment. I don't have an assistant answering my calls, I work on projects before I respond to e-mails, and I am frequently unavailable from 2:00 to 3:00 p.m. for school pickup. So many women — so many people — are choosing to work from home. Clients and businesses are broadening their view of this and modifying their expectations — not expecting less from us in terms of the quality of our work, but being more understanding of our alternative work environments. I'm delighted that I'm able to tackle my own business from home!

Maintaining a Professional Image

How do you put your best business foot forward when you might be working from home in your pajamas? Even though one part of you might be a harried mom or panicked mom-to-be, you need to learn how to project professionalism, whether at home or out in public.

Yes, we are moms. Yes, we love that we get to work from home (occasionally in our PJs and yoga pants). Yes, the coffee is great, and our coworkers are mostly easy to deal with, especially when they nap when they are supposed to and don't make strange noises when we're on the phone.

But we're talking business here. If you want to be taken seriously, you have to take yourself and your company seriously. Here are some things to think about in order to establish business parameters within your household to help project a more professional image:

1) Set office hours to take calls when your children are napping or in school.
2) Take meetings outside of the home — your local Panera or Starbucks would be happy to "host" you and your client.
3) For out-of-the-house meetings, have two go-to outfits at the ready that make you feel fabulous (and do not include spandex).
4) Reschedule any meetings that might be interrupted by sick children, or for those other all-important times when you need to wear your "Mom" hat.
5) Unless it is prearranged and you know you can swing it, do not take your children with you to these meetings (even if you are sure they will color quietly).
6) Work when the house is quiet. This might mean really early in the morning or late into the night. Carve out that productive time, and use it well.
7) If you need additional hours in the day, consider hiring a nanny or mother's

helper — even for a few mornings a week. Don't fritter that time away if you do get it.

8) DO NOT use your children as an excuse for incomplete work or delayed projects. You want your clients to think of you as a business owner, not as a woman distracted by the goings-on in her life.

"Coming from someone who hasn't had a mother-in-law living nearby to take care of my children, I recognize that paying for a nanny is an investment in this period of time in my life," explains Janice Croze of 5 Minutes for Mom. "Professionalism is key. You have to make your clients feel as if this is a real business."

Cheryl Lockhart of International Strategies started out with a part-time nanny in the home. "I realized very early on that there was no way I could get anything done except when my children were sleeping or otherwise occupied."

Cheryl says that actually spending some of the money she earns on a nanny gives her additional motivation to get her work done, and helps her to value her own time more. "If I'm paying her, I know I have to make at least that much in the time that she is here. I'm more focused and can take my 'mommy hat' off and put on my 'business hat.'"

Promoting Yourself

Many of us are afraid to promote ourselves. Embrace the fact that you really are allowed to promote yourself. Acknowledge the fact that you are good at the job you have chosen and the path you have taken to start your business. If you do not believe that someone should hire you or buy your products, you shouldn't be doing what you're doing. You have to start everything from a strong belief in yourself, or else why should anyone else believe in you, do business with you, or buy from you?

Before Jerilyn Winstead had officially launched her high-quality swimmable mermaid costumes business, Aquatails.com, she decided she would need to do something big to get herself and her business noticed.

Says Jerilyn, "I boldly called the Denver Aquarium and asked them if they would like mermaids in their aquarium. Turns out they had already been wanting mermaids, so the owner had me and my team come up twice over the winter to demo 'mermaiding' in the aquarium. In the process, we got permission to do our first ever photo shoot at the aquarium, and we then used the photos and videos to launch our Web site! The aquarium then went on to develop their own mermaid show, and we showed them the way. So now can I take credit for the mermaid show at the Denver Aquarium?"

Aliza on self-promotion

I've been accused of being a self-promoter as if it were a bad thing. Guys do it all the time, but when a woman stands up and says, "Here are my accomplishments," often the loudest detractors are other women. We need to be supportive of and promote each other, but first and foremost, we need to start with supporting and promoting ourselves. I'm here to tell you, this isn't easy.

I may appear on lots of blogs or in the media or on stage, but there is always a little voice inside me saying, "Who do you think you are?" For every time I feel empowered and confident, there are countless times that I shy away from opportunities because I'm not feeling worthy. Life is too short to listen to the naysayers or your own inner critic that keeps you from proudly announcing who you are and what you do.

Danielle on self-promotion

I have had a difficult time with this. I have stood in front of crowds, introducing myself with only my name and Web site, forgetting entirely that I should be sharing WHY I'm the person who SHOULD be speaking to the audience about any given topic. No, they don't want an itemized resume. No, they don't want to hear me name-drop for an hour, but they DO need to know WHY they should be listening to me.

My husband says he sits in the back of the room, wondering, "Why don't you tell them you are writing a book?" and "Why don't you tell them you've been on national television?" But for some reason, I've hesitated — likely because of the exact scenario Aliza mentioned. I've always been fearful of being accused of overly promoting myself. But the truth is, I DO have a right to be proud of what I have accomplished. And the work I have done is what makes me qualified for the next project, the next client.

Tell people why you deserve their attention and their business. List your accomplishments. Hire someone else to fill in the kudos and positive words. Let someone else read your bio or your company "About Us" page, and spice it up to better position you as the expert that you are, or to highlight your products as the awesome things they are. Because it is often so much easier for someone else to talk about the good things you're doing than it is for you to do it yourself, turn to others to push you past your aversion to self-promotion. Once you see what they've written about you or heard what they've said about your business, accept the compliments. OWN your experience, your accomplishments, your skills and talents.

OK, now let's take a look at some more ways you can build your brand, gain credibility, and increase your exposure.

I think all of us need to do ourselves a favor and invest in the time to craft our brand, our image, our 30-second elevator pitch, etc., so that when someone asks us what we do, we have a short, simple, powerful answer.

—Lara Galloway, Mom Biz Academy

Online Marketing Tactics

We aren't here to tell you that traditional print advertising is dead. We don't believe it is, but we do think there is a time and place for it. Since you are starting up a new business, this may not be the time and place for buying a newspaper ad in your local paper. You want to keep your costs to a minimum, so let's focus on the outlets that provide the biggest returns for the least amount of money. Much of what we are going to suggest is free or available for a minimal cost.

We've already talked about social media marketing and how using those tools takes time and effort as you form relationships and engage in conversations. Most customers expect to be able to interact with companies and business owners through social media these days, but the following are other marketing tactics you can use in conjunction with social media. Always consider your audience — whom you are trying to reach and what you want them to do — before you start marketing.

Guest Blogging

One way to get your name out there and showcase your expertise is to write and submit guest blog posts to blogs that reach your target market. To get started, think of the topics you can write about that are timely, compelling, and effectively show others what you know. Craft the posts not as mini-commercials but as useful information with a strong point of view. Then contact the editors or owners of blogs that publish posts related to your topics of interest, and offer them your guest post. Or you can do the reverse and find the blogs where you'd like to have a presence, then craft a post compatible with their content and submit it to them. Many blogs will accept guest posts if you submit well-thought-out and well-written posts that fit their blog's theme and tone. Some highly trafficked and popular blogs where you can submit a blog post, but that have a stringent vetting process, include The Huffington Post (for topics ranging from business and tech to media and entertainment) and Mashable (which focuses more on tech and business). Guest blogging is typically done for free and for the marketing value. Most blog posts include a short bio at the end, sometimes with a link that can serve as a marketing tool for you and your company.

E-newsletters

Sending electronic newsletters or e-newsletters can be an inexpensive way to reach your customers and clients, to keep them up-to-date on your latest products and services. You can include several articles, in your e-newsletter to showcase your expertise; however, keep them shorter than you might on a blog or Web site. You can also include headlines and summaries of articles, then link to the full text on your Web site or blog. You can convert readers to buyers by offering coupons or loyalty discounts, as well as providing content specific to your industry. When using an electronic newsletter service like Constant Contact, iContact, or MailChimp, you can access reports to gauge your subscribers' interest in what you're sending out, based on the number of people who open your e-mail and click on the links. Additionally, this regular communication — usually monthly — gives you the opportunity to keep the conversation going with potential customers and follow up on potential leads. To use iContact will run you $19 a month for up to 1,000 subscribers, and Constant Contact charges $15 for up to 500, and then $30 for 501 to 2,500. MailChimp has a helpful free version and is fun and easy to use.

Directory Listings

Just about every industry has specific directories online where people can find businesses in addition to using general searchable directories and search engines. The goals for listing your business in online directories are to drive traffic to your site and to create more presence for your business on the Web. Listing your site is free in many cases, although it does take time to find the appropriate directories to use. Many of these sites let you include pictures of products or allow you to list your individual services. Once you're listed, let your customers know and invite them to post reviews. Some popular directory options include Yahoo! Local, Google Local, Google Places, Facebook Places, Best of the Web, Bing Local, HotFrog.com, Merchant Circle, and Yelp. Don't forget location-based social networks as well, such as Foursquare and GoWalla.

Facebook Ads

Though traditional advertising might not always be effective or might be too expensive to use when you're first starting a business, there are some very affordable options online for advertising, including Facebook ads. These ads let you specifically target the people you want to reach — the ideal client or customer for your business — based on gender, age, location, relationship status, education, and more. While you pay more if your ads are more targeted, depending on your criteria your ads could cost around 50 cents to over $1 per click or CPC (when people click on your ads) or even less for impressions or CPM (when people just see your ad). Facebook ads are totally customizable, giving you greater control even after you've posted them, so if you need to change them in the middle of an ad run, you can. You can use these ads to drive traffic to your Facebook fan page or to any page on the Web, including your Web site or blog. Budgeting for these ads is fairly simple; specify how much you want to spend per day, such as $20, and as soon as enough people have seen or clicked on your ads, they stop appearing until the next day and will only run for the number of days you specify.

Google Adwords

With Google Adwords, you pay only for clicks, meaning that you pay each time someone clicks on your ad. You can set a maximum budget for each day. There is no minimum ad buy, and you can choose to stop your campaign at any time. You can "bid" on keyword placement as well. This means that you can pay to have your ad show up when people search for specific words on Google. Be careful: choosing a popular word like "travel" and buying top placement can get expensive, running more than $50 per click.

Mobile Advertising

You can purchase ads that appear on mobile phones, usually embedded in mobile apps and games or appearing on the mobile Web. There are many solutions for purchasing mobile ads, including Google's AdMob and JumpTap. Often, the best use of mobile advertising is to promote your own mobile app, but if you don't have one, you can also drive traffic to your site and build brand awareness. Make sure your Web site is mobile friendly by using services such as Mobify or MoFuse for free or for a montly fee. Mobile ads are a fraction of the size of traditional ads. Most mobile ad networks and agencies can help you develop the ad copy and art or take what you've drafted and optimize it for the mobile medium.

Offline Marketing Tactics

We're going to throw in a few ideas for ways you can build your brand offline. Not all of these will suit you, but they can be effective ways to reach potential customers and increase your profile.

Bylined Article

If you're a writer — or if you can afford to hire a freelance writer to craft an article based on your thoughts — you could give this content to a variety of outlets and gain exposure through the "byline," which is the credit given to you for writing it. Common places that will accept bylined articles include print newsletters from organizations, associations, churches, synagogues, and chambers of commerce. Some local or community newspapers also accept bylined articles. Who else is sending you newsletters? Check out your local utility company, your neighborhood grocery store, and even other businesses. The key to these articles is that they are not commercials for your company, but instead are about interesting topics and include useful information that the publisher of a newsletter or newspaper wants to share with readers. Some popular formats for these articles include "top ten tips" and lists of dos and don'ts.

Public Speaking

If you're an extrovert, public speaking is a phenomenal way to both build your brand and market yourself, especially for service providers. Every time you take advantage of an opportunity to speak in front of an audience, you are positioning yourself as an expert on that specific topic. If you've never done any public speaking, get as much presentation experience as you can by volunteering to speak at local businesses and networking events, including your local chamber of commerce and trade associations. As you establish a comfort level in front of a group, you can continue to expand your audiences. If you have more speaking experience, try to get into social media events such as TedX — a local version of the venerable TED conference — or Ignite, an event involving rapid six-minute-long presentations with interesting slide shows. These events are videotaped, so you can add the video of your presentation to your site. You can watch other people's presentations on the Web sites for Ted Talks, TedX, and Ignite.

Public Relations

You can also use public relations to promote your business, usually by building relationships with reporters and news producers to encourage them to tell your story in their media outlet. Sending out press releases can still be a useful tactic to help you get the word out, although now you can enhance a traditional press release with links to your social networks, embedded photographs, audio clips, and video. Use a site like PitchEngine to build social media releases quickly and easily. If you have the budget, hiring a PR professional could be a good investment to free you up to work more on your business.

There are so many other ways, big and small, that you can build your brand. Visit MomIncorporated.com for more affordable ideas that you can put to use today.

Tell everyone you know about what you are doing. Don't be afraid of "failure," because success is always right around the corner from an "oh, no, it's never going to work" period!

—Lisa Cottrell-Bentley, Do Life Right, Inc.

Chapter 8
Our Business, Ourselves

You are so close to taking a dive right off the deep end and into the business of your dreams. As you have read each page, we hope that you have been taking notes and are already formulating your business plan, your brand, and some of your strategies.

Venturing out on your own to start a business from home is no easy task. We know that. It takes passion, energy, a love of family, a belief in yourself, a respect for your new business, and a commitment to develop a plan and make it happen.

Take to heart a favorite quote of ours:

"Do one thing every day that scares you...."
— Eleanor Roosevelt

We encourage you to start your journey, and join the millions of women who are destined to do it on their own. Like them, you can find a way to care for your families and create viable businesses. Know that this might scare you daily — but the rewards can be amazing.

For additional inspiration, we want to highlight some women who have hung the entrepreneurial shingle outside their homes, who have changed diapers while on conference calls, who have ignored the need for sleep in favor of "just a little more productivity," who have battled the guilt that comes with choosing work over family on a Saturday and family over work on a Tuesday, who have invested more time than they ever thought existed, who have scoffed at the idea of balance yet somehow found the time to see their six-year-old score her first soccer goal and still meet that business deadline by end of day.

The women we interviewed are all different. Some sell products, others offer services. Some do business locally, while others have created an international presence. But they all have something in common: they all started in the same place — their homes. They started while pregnant or while caring for a newborn or with small children running around at home. And they all started with the same things: an idea, a passion, and a belief that they could succeed.

On with the interviews!

Amy Ormond, Founder • Wooster & Prince

www.woosterandprince.com

Amy Ormond founded Wooster & Prince as a stationery and paper goods line featuring her vintage textile-inspired designs. She launched her business at the National Stationery Show in May 2003, after nearly a year of planning. At that time, her older son, Jack, was two years old and her younger son, Bear, was six months.

As the Wooster & Prince brand grew, Amy began to license her artwork to other companies. Today, her company has multiple licensing agreements with partners in a range of industries, and her designs can be seen on paper goods, gifts, textiles, tabletop, home décor, and many more applications. She considers her business to be her "third child," as it came along at the same time as her children and has required an equal amount of work and attention.

What inspired Amy to start her company?

"I have had a lifetime love of entrepreneurism and design, but had never given myself the opportunity to pursue these two passions simultaneously," says Amy.

After she left her position as a marketing executive and consultant after the birth of her first son, Amy says she had time to think about what truly gave her a sense of fulfillment.

Says Amy, "Until then, I had been mostly a 'weekend artist,'" creating oil paintings in her family's loft (on Wooster and Prince streets in SoHo, New York City), a huge open space with no walls to separate work spaces from living, sleeping, and play spaces. There were simply no physical or even visual boundaries anywhere in the loft.

Amy quickly learned that having wet oil canvases around her apartment was not very conducive to having two little ones running around. So she taught herself how to use Adobe Illustrator, a software application for drawing and creating. By switching her creative tools, new doors opened for Amy, allowing her to pursue her art and the designs that would eventually become the heart of her business.

Even as she worked out her workspace issues, Amy faced other challenges. During the first three years of launching her business with two toddler boys in her midst, Amy suffered enormously from insomnia.

"At the time, I recall thinking that it was actually awfully convenient that I was running on less than four hours of sleep a night, as it allowed me to get more work done and speak to my vendors in China in real time," says Amy. "But over time, a level of exhaustion set in that was pervasive in everything I tried or wanted to do."

Amy reveals that it was tough for her to admit that she had to address the fact that, although she was getting immense satisfaction from her growing family and business, she was neglecting her own well-being.

"I made changes in my life — more and better sleep and exercise — that vastly improved the balance in my life," she says. "And now I feel I'm a better person, mother, business owner, and wife for having done it. "

The bulk of Amy's first five years in business consisted of working from home. She also intermittently rented spaces in shared artist lofts and other small places to get out of her home and have some elbow room.

During this time, her family moved out of New York City to a house in the country. Amy's workspace was a dark and damp basement for a year while her boys were in preschool. The basement wasn't ideal for keeping her sons within earshot, but she didn't change her work environment until her basement flooded during a storm and she nearly lost all of her work. She then moved to her very first studio two miles from her home.

Amy is a big proponent of getting help; she hired babysitters and mother's helpers at first, then eventually a part-time nanny.

"As I began to do more trade shows that required being away from home, having a dependable nanny was crucial," Amy explains. "My husband has been incredibly supportive and helps out a great deal, despite his having a very demanding career as well."

Amy says she learned early on that in order to make her business a reality, she would need to work when her boys slept, which often meant very early in the morning and very late at night.

"I realized that although I was embarking on a creative endeavor, building a successful business was as much about being organized and deliberate as anything else," she says. "These are skills that most mothers either have or acquire quickly with small children, and so I put them to good use with my business."

Amy's boys are now eight and nine, and she has found that, as with most things in life, the only constant is change.

"Any attempt I have made to anticipate long-term childcare situations and needs has been a futile effort. A child's needs ebb and flow and, like a business, require flexibility and creativity in how you manage it," she says.

Amy told us she is still striving for success and feels she is a long way from fully realizing it. She circles back to what she learned long ago, after her first son was born: that the key to having gotten this far was to have defined and embraced what it was that brought her real fulfillment.

Says Amy, "For me, it was being an entrepreneur and an artist. Once I had this clear in my mind and heart, I simply set myself a goal and a deadline for combining these passions and talents into a business. I never wavered from the goal and never let myself off the hook for meeting those deadlines. After all, I was finally answering to my true self."

Tobi Kosanke, Founder • Crazy K Farm Pet and Poultry Products
www.crazykfarm.com

As a petroleum geologist with a flexible telecommuting work schedule, Tobi Kosanke was successfully balancing a well-paying career with caring for her child, who had a medical issue from the day she was born. Tobi worked mostly at home until her daughter was four. Then, her new manager forced her to make a decision: care for her daughter at home or work in the office. Tobi chose her daughter.

Tobi's family farm was taking in rescued livestock and poultry — nearly 200 of them — and covering their mounting bills after a 60 percent drop in income was impossible.

"I was unable to find another position with a flexible work arrangement that would enable me to care for my daughter," Tobi recalls. "So I decided to start a home-based business to manufacture and sell unique items I had invented for our own animals."

Crazy K Farm Pet and Poultry Products, LLC, manufactures useful items that improve the quality of life of pets and backyard chickens, including the patented Hen Saver® hen apron, which protects hens from treading by roosters, pecking from other hens, and also furnishes some protection against chicken hawks. Other products include the Avian Haven® hut for parrots and other caged birds, and several products that are patent-pending, including the Kitty Holster® cat harness, Hen Holster® chicken diaper and harness, and Birdy Bra® crop supporter and chest protector. Each item was invented by Tobi and tested by her livestock.

"I did not start out with the goal of becoming an entrepreneur," says Tobi. "I'm a prime example of the saying 'Necessity is the mother of invention.'"

Tobi's business was started with two loans: one from a bank and the other from a credit union. With the bank, she refinanced her car, and at the credit union, she received a personal line of credit. Later, she boosted business growth with a loan from cousins.

As her business grew, she began to struggle with working too many hours away from her child. She did manage to cook dinner for her family after a full day of working and feeding the farm animals, but found herself running upstairs to her home office as her husband did the dishes and bathed their daughter.

"Time and again I would promise her I'd put her to bed, but by the time I made it back downstairs, she'd be asleep," says Tobi. "I knew this could not continue, so I created a schedule and stuck to it."

Tobi began turning her computer completely off to make it harder to run back upstairs to "check one last e-mail" or complete "one last little task." She confesses that, at the time, she was sure her business would come crashing down around her if she didn't get everything finished that she thought needed to be done.

"I was pleasantly surprised to learn that it is unlikely that irreparable damage can occur by not working after 6:00 p.m., and what few minor disasters did occur (that could have been averted if I had worked until midnight), were, in fact, very manageable," Tobi says.

Eventually, she found the right schedule and rhythm for herself and her family.

To get a better handle on her business growth, Tobi turned to her local Small Business Development Center and received guidance from a business counselor who checked her numbers.

"I know pet products. I invent them, and they are selling well," says Tobi. "But even though I'm highly educated with a doctorate in geology, that did not translate into knowing how to run a business."

At her company's two-year mark, Tobi realized she was growing faster than she could handle. Around the same time, she entered and won a business-pitch contest and was awarded six weeks of free business coaching.

"My coach is my lifeline," says Tobi. "My biggest regret is that I did not start with a business coach from day one. I recommend that any mom starting a business save herself a lot of anguish, frustration, and struggles with self-doubt by hiring a qualified business coach as soon as she forms her business. It is money well spent."

These days, Tobi is comfortable being "president of Crazy K Farm," but when her daughter comes home from school, she's "Mom." When her daughter is home for holidays and summers, Tobi is much more disciplined about the blocks of time she is president of her company and the blocks of time she's all mom.

"There is no multitasking that will efficiently enable me to be both every minute of the day. I tried that and it was a lose-lose situation," says Tobi. "I accept that, and I am growing Crazy K Farm on my schedule."

Selena Cuffe, Founder • Heritage Link Brands
www.heritagelinkbrands.com

It was a professor at Harvard Business School that ultimately gave Selena Cuffe the words that would someday shape her journey as an entrepreneur. He told her to take note of the things in life that "stop you in your tracks, that piss you off, that get you excited — for THIS will be what you have passion for." After a trip to South Africa in 2005, Selena realized that despite a booming wine industry in the region, 85 percent of South Africans were excluded from reaping the benefits of the wine they produced. Selena leveraged her marketing and corporate background from P&G and founded Heritage Link Brands, a venture that merged her passions for entrepreneurship and social justice. She was pregnant with the first of her two boys when she began the process of launching her business from home.

HLB is now the largest importer and marketer of black-produced wine from Africa. With the help of her husband, Selena's company partners with indigenous producers previously disenfranchised by South Africa's system of apartheid to develop, promote, and manage a portfolio of internationally renowned, award-winning wine brands. Their wines allow customers to "drink well while doing good."

In college, Selena was involved in a very serious car accident, but knew she was spared for a reason. That reason, she believes, was to create this very business. "This was serendipitous," she laughs. She had been working in the corporate world, but knew she wanted to do something entrepreneurial. "I knew I wanted to build a brand that would outlive me, and I was on a quest to figure out what to do." She continues, "During that trip to South Africa in 2005, I found it."

But this new venture was not without challenges. Selena realized fairly quickly that her career choice was based on passion, not on a knowledge of wine. "I was trying to penetrate an industry I knew nothing about. There was a learning curve and a need for a lot of research," she says.

Making the situation even more complicated was Selena's fear of running a core business (wine) that could be harmful to her soon-to-be-born child.

"As a pregnant woman, I couldn't taste the wine, and what would I do about breastfeeding?" she asked. She resolved her issue with a lot of spitting, swirling, asking opinions, and forming focus groups.

With nearly a half-dozen years of business under her belt, Selena is now able to reflect on what she may have done differently if given the opportunity to start her business over again. She elaborates, "If I had it to do over again, I would have taken even more time. Even though we took a full year for product development, I still would have waited longer for our launch."

Like many of us, Selena worries about money. "I would have financed our operation differently. There are days that I think I have put our family in a precarious position, since we are invested in the business."

Being able to manage both a flourishing business and the family she loves takes effort, and Selena credits her husband for helping her. "This business works because I am married to my husband. The secret to successfully juggling my business and family responsibilities is following my golden rule: Family First." In fact, for Selena, the ability to follow this rule means she is not only sane, but also healthy. "My business relationships have only been that much richer when I am mindful about keeping my family first. When my home and family are healthy, I am healthy. When I am healthy — mind, body, and soul — I am then perfectly poised to nurture business relationships."

And she recommends that those of you reading this book — you moms and soon-to-be-moms who are getting ready to follow your passions — make sure you, too, have support.

She is adamant, "If you don't have a supportive spouse, don't do it! Entrepreneurship is the antithesis of balance — you need others who can support you mentally and physically." And don't forget about YOU. "When putting family first, remember that you are an important member of the family. If you take care of yourself first, you will have that much more energy for the rest of your family."

Sheena Edwards, Founder • Lizzie Lou Shoes
www.lizzieloushoes.com

Sheena Edwards has always done "something" when it came to work, but the urge to venture out on her own simply wouldn't go away. She had dabbled in jewelry, toys, even home goods, but nothing felt like the "thing" she needed to drive her passion. But in July of 2008, things changed. Her then two-and-a-half-year-old daughter handed her a pair of flip-flops. Though gorgeous, the price tag was over $200. A lightbulb went off in Sheena's mind. With a cousin in India experienced in manufacturing goods who was also "searching" for the right opportunity, and a belief that women deserved stylish and affordable items that made them feel good about themselves, Sheena began down the road to what is now Lizzie Lou Shoes. Even though Sheena didn't have a lot of money to invest, she and her cousin began to research manufacturers, sending samples back and forth. With only a Web site, no PR or advertising, and with three children (ages two, six, and nine), Sheena "gave birth" to Lizzie Lou Shoes in May of 2009.

Sheena knew that starting this business would be a way for her to fulfill a passion outside of her role as mom. "It was most important to me to stay home when my children were little, to be here when they got off the bus. I want to be available when they become teens. And I was inspired by the idea that I knew there was a marketplace for quality shoes that made women feel beautiful yet were affordable."

But even as the pieces began to fall into place — the passion for shoes, her faith in her cousin's experience and connections — there were still challenges. Sheena reflects, "My first shipment was a mess. I paid too much for shipping. At least 50 to 75 of the pairs of flip-flops were useless. So I simply had to try to recoup my money." By 2010, the following year, Sheena had fixed most of the problems. "We had better leather, a better sole, better crystals."

However, she still wishes she could go back and do a few things differently. "We didn't know shoes. I wish we had initially hired someone to help us with importing. It would have cost us less in the long run," she explains.

And don't think starting a business is a piece of cake. Sheena asserts very strongly, "You have to love it. This is a labor of love. If I didn't walk into my closet and see 20 pairs of flip-flops I loved, I would have quit, because at 10 at night, I'm tired, and sometimes you have to keep going. If you don't love it, you won't keep going."

Understanding your limitations is part of this. Sheena suggests knowing how much money and time you are willing to commit *before* you actually begin. And, make sure your plans are in place. "I would also have started smaller. Maybe brought in 50 shoes, worked on test marketing, or have given some shoes away, as compared to starting with one large shipment that ended up costing so much money and having so many problems."

Sheena estimates she may have spent $2,000 to $3,000 to have someone experienced help with importing and shipping, but it would have saved her the $2,000 to $3,000 she lost to mistakes.

But even after all of this time, and having sold hundreds of pairs of shoes, Sheena doesn't reply with a resounding "YES!" when asked if Lizzie Lou (the business itself) is a success. She pauses, then says, "It's yes and no. I think in the spring of 2010, my line and styles were perfect. We had some problems with shoes in the first line and second, but by the third line everything was good, no problems. As far as success I think, yes, I hit the mark on a great product — comfortable, high quality, and great designs." But on the other hand, she is torn regarding some of the actual business aspects. "No on publicity, marketing, and branding. I wanted everything perfect before I hit it hard with promotion. But then a bad economy hit. Along with little funding, I decided to do it all on my own." Sheena will soon be featured in *People StyleWatch* magazine, has a new relationship with SolesforSouls, and hopes these will be just the tipping point she needs to feel Lizzie Lou's success all the way down to her toes.

Sheena's love of being a mompreneur keeps her going. "I really enjoy being a mom and I love the title. It is a good feeling to know I can be home with my kids and that they can learn from my business. I feel like I'm teaching them and fulfilling my passion. It makes me a better mom."

And that happiness translates into a two-fold success for Sheena: "First, owning my own business, designing and wearing my own shoe line, and sharing them with family and friends." But even more than that is the benefit to her family. "I'm able to do all of this and still be home with my three kids, Emily, eleven, Lizzie, eight, and Vince, four."

Nika Stewart, Founder • The LapTop Mom
www.laptopmom.com

In 2005, Nika Stewart was hit by something unexpected — depression. It struck just three weeks after she had her first child, a daughter. Having always been an entrepreneur, Nika decided to turn this struggle into something positive. The idea for her current business, The LapTop Mom, came to Nika during this difficult time. She had been a successful interior designer, but was struggling to satisfy clients and to spend the time she wanted with her daughter. After realizing that women didn't have to choose between being with their children and running a business, she began to teach them how to take their work online. Thus, The LapTop Mom was born. Nika now speaks and coaches moms on how to master a flexible schedule that allows them to enjoy both a career and motherhood.

"I couldn't go back to the way things were. I wanted both freedom and flexibility, and I wanted to build what I wanted to build around my priority — my little angel at home. That translated into creating something online." Nika's online work includes teleseminars, personal coaching, even a "boot camp" — all designed to give moms the opportunity to feel the peace and serenity of work and family she felt while coming to terms with balancing both her new daughter and a career she loved.

This meant tapping into the support system she had at home, her husband, and considering other options. "It was a Catch-22. I needed more time to work on my business. So I needed my husband to help more. But I wasn't making the money. And he was. But if I wasn't spending time on the business, I wouldn't have the opportunity to get the business to grow. What would a man do? He would hire help. Get a babysitter. Do what it takes."

Nika recommends choosing a path that allows you both flexibility and the opportunity to leverage your own talents.

"You need to be flexible as a mom, and you don't want your business to suffer if you need to take care of family priorities. By finding ways to leverage, you can reach more people and make more money — without working more hours." This may sound like it's easier said than done, but Nika has some suggestions. "Instead of working only one-on-one, teach a class to 20 people at the same time. Record your class and sell it as a product to people all over the world. Transcribe your recording and create a new product. Keep looking for ways to repurpose your information, and you can multiply the impact of what you are doing in business — so you can spread your brilliance to more people and make more money, while remaining flexible and free to take care of your family and yourself."

Nika considers her ability to manage multiple streams of passive income one of her keys to success — that and running what she calls a freedom-based business. "The key to my personal success is building and running a business that supports my ideal lifestyle."

How does this "passive income" work? Nika is happy to explain: "It is the money that comes in AFTER we are done working. So instead of doing the traditional 'trading time for money,' we do the work once, and get paid for weeks, months, and years later. Orders come in for my products while I am sleeping, out with a friend, or taking my daughter to school. The money goes into our bank account, the product is automatically delivered to the client, and we don't even have to be in our office for this all to work smoothly. The process is automated."

For Nika, it is her "information products" that provide this additional income, including her "How to Produce Your Own Teleseminar" newsletters and articles, and a seven-part recorded series where she teaches women how to begin to create and sell their own online products. For the series, she had the recordings transcribed, added worksheets and templates, had professional graphics created, put the recordings on CDs, and had a three-ring binder produced to house the transcripts and action sheets. This is now selling as her LapTop Mom SUCCESS System Home Study Course.

Since she has already done the work to create the product, she can now just enjoy earning income on it — over and over.

Nika says with a smile, "My favorite experience is waking up in the morning, opening up my computer, and seeing sales that occurred during the night. I am literally making money in my sleep!"

Nika also recommends hiring help before you think you are ready — especially since we *rarely* think we have reached that point. She remembers getting started. "I struggled for too long alone, thinking that I needed to do it all myself. But no ultrasuccessful person does it alone. I have learned to delegate, hire coaches and mentors, and outsource parts of my business that are not my brilliance."

Nika says she wishes she had a time machine. "If I could go back in time, I would have done this early on, and saved myself years of headache, loneliness, and feeling overwhelmed."

For Nika, being an entrepreneur meant creating the life she wanted. "I knew how I wanted to live — FIRST — and then I built a business model that supports that. I get to be a hands-on mommy and spread my message globally while earning a great income."

Alli Worthington, Chief Creative Officer • Blissdom Events
www.alliworthington.com

Alli Worthington is a living example of how to Go Big and find your bliss. In 2007, she started a blog. In 2008, she founded Blissfully Domestic, a community site with the overarching goal of bringing good things to women — in the form of articles, news, and interesting opportunities. Today, that overall goal still rings true. She is now the cofounder of BlissDom Events as well as the cofounder and chief creative officer of BlissDom, the second largest women's conference in the country — and the first one to go international.

Just how does this mother of five young boys manage to pull that off, work tirelessly, and maintain her sanity? She sticks with a personal motto, "Do the most good for the most people." This includes the women she hopes to inspire and, naturally, her family. Also, she refuses to operate from a place of fear.

She elaborates, "I am not afraid to fail. It is one of the reasons for my success. I will happily try something. If I fail, I say, 'Well, that was a terrible idea,' then I dust myself off and try something else."

Her lack of fear likely comes from life experiences — many that haven't been easy. At one point, her husband lost his job, the market crashed, and Alli and her family lost their home. Much of her journey was chronicled on her original blog, Mrs. Fussypants. Having successfully picked herself up from that trying time, she has found her story to be a source of inspiration for many women struggling through similar circumstances. And that period of her life has also inspired a future goal: Alli smiles as she explains, "My long-term goal . . . well, I want to make it possible for at least 25 women to work within their homes. I want to help them to pursue life on their own terms and feel financially stable." Much as Alli, herself, does now.

When Alli first decided to start her own business, she knew only two things: she didn't want her family to be dependent on only one income, and she wanted to provide financial security for her family. Much as Danielle recounted in Chapter 1, Alli started with a dream and faith in herself.

With only $27 to dedicate to this new endeavor, Alli dove in. She remembers, "Right after I learned to attach a photo to an e-mail, I started a blog. I used a laptop with missing keys." And that isn't all. She made herself a student of all things on the Internet. "I stayed up late," she says. "I watched YouTube tutorials and I read blogs."

Alli stresses that no matter what, take the business side of this seriously. She explains,

"Business advice needs to be sought out, and researched." On the list of people you need in your life, according to Alli: an accountant — especially one who understands the specifics of working online, if that is your chosen profession — and definitely a lawyer.

Alli says she now knows that to do her best requires some outside help, whether it is in her office or home. "For every woman out there, my advice is to find the money in your budget to get help — simply for your sanity. For me, this has made all the difference."

Janice Croze, Cofounder • 5 Minutes for Mom
www.5minutesformom.com

Janice Croze is one of the twin bloggers behind the übersuccessful mom-community Web site, 5 Minutes for Mom. Janice started working online doing network marketing in 2003, when her son was only one, and her twin sister, Susan, was struggling with infertility. In partnership with their mom, Janice and Susan started e-commerce stores in 2004, then decided to start a blog in January of 2006. At the time, Susan was a software developer and knew she wouldn't want to be working 12-hour days once there was a baby in her life. And Janice realized that she desperately needed to be the boss of her own time. She reflects, "Ultimately, my kids come first and I need to work around parenting. I needed a vehicle to be creative that had adult time and gave me energy to be with my kids."

After researching the blogosphere, Susan came up with the name 5 Minutes for Mom, and they officially launched their community site in March of 2006, long before anything of its kind existed in the online space. Janice and Susan had baby girls two weeks apart a little more than a year later, in the fall of 2007.

5 Minutes for Mom felt like the natural next step. Janice remembers, "We wanted to create a place to promote and support the online mom community. It is a hybrid of a site. It took off because of the altruistic goal to help moms succeed and to empower and support each other — that is a force."

Janice and Susan are two of the most well-known moms in the online space, but despite the appearance of over-the-top success, their journey has not been without challenges — namely money. As in, there have been years without making any.

"Building a site takes time. We needed to build our page rank, and our traffic, for one to two years. We were fortunate that our husbands paid the bills, but it was a challenge getting them to understand," Janice explains. "We only began to pay ourselves a salary in 2010. Until then, we reinvested everything we made in our business. Our overhead has been high — we have put tens of thousands of dollars into our business — in staff, travel, hosting, and development."

For Janice and Susan, this business works for a few reasons, not the least of which is teamwork. Janice says, "In my whole life, I can't do it all on my own. I am stronger with people around me — it allows me to be bigger than myself."

Having that support system and the ability to be rational about the process is what Janice believes has allowed her and her sister to experience the success of 5 Minutes for Mom.

"Be realistic about your goals. Starting a business with a baby might be very challenging, so recognize that it won't be easy, and try to plan for it," she says. "Spend time building your product before trying to sell it. Set up a support system — you will need it. Hire very carefully — and before you think you need to. Don't wait until you think you are 'profitable' to hire the help you need. By then you will be behind."

One of the things we love about Janice and Susan is their ability to embrace their journey. When asked what they would change about the process of starting their business, assuming they could go back in time, they simply say, "Nothing."

Janice reflects, "I really respect the way we did it. We put our noses to the ground and decided to worry about the money later. We focused on building something we were proud of. Our goal was not to make money that year, but to build a successful business." Janice knows what she wants. "I'm not working for a salary. I'm working for a future."

Wendy Piersall, Founder • Woo Jr. Kids Activities
www.wendypiersall.com

Reinvention and the desire to keep learning and evolving have been the core motivation behind Wendy Piersall's success and desire to be an entrepreneur. Having been raised by an entrepreneurial father, Wendy didn't know any other path, but she alone can take the credit for actually making it all happen.

In 1994, at only 26 years old, Wendy, a brand-new mom, made a decision that would set her on the path to where she is today. She says, "It was faith and determination. I knew I had to do whatever I could to be with my baby. This was a leap of faith."

It was at this time that she started a craft business — the first of many endeavors Wendy would tackle and make a success. From this business, Wendy started a social networking site for personal development for women, eMomsathome.com. At the time, she figured there may be one or two moms who might be interested in what she had to say about starting an Internet business from home. "I didn't consider myself an expert, I just planned to show women what I had learned on this journey," she explains.

Emoms turned into a blog network, and then Wendy rebranded it as Sparkplugging and sold it. In 2009, Woo Jr. Kids Activities was born, a network of Web sites for kids, teachers, and parents. The site includes activities, printables, coloring pages, and dozens of other resources.

Now, Wendy can add "author" to her resume with her book, *Mom Blogging for Dummies,* which was released in summer 2011.

Wendy recognizes that working on what she loves is easier now that her children are a bit older — her youngest is in third grade. "When you are working for yourself and from home, there is no separation between family and work. When you feel like you are caught up on family, you realize you are behind on work, and when you are caught up on work, you feel as though you have neglected your family."

Wendy continues, "The hardest part of the process is knowing when you have crossed the line, and you typically don't see it until you are out of balance." She suggests being realistic about what you can expect from yourself. "I always thought I could do more than I really could. The guilt is paralyzing. So go easy on yourself. I don't necessarily know how to make that happen, but I wish I had done it."

And, of course, the second hardest part is getting the money and cash flow right.

It is on the topic of finance and cash flow that Wendy offers one of her most important pieces of advice. Though she wouldn't go back and change any part of her process, as she feels each step has been part of a valuable lesson, she does have a suggestion: "Learn how to have a stable income."

How do you do this? Do as Wendy has done and make yourself a student of your craft. Whenever there was something Wendy didn't understand, anything that she thought she might be able to do better, she put herself in a position to learn. She says, "The best way to explain it is: don't get so hyperfocused on one way to make money. Consider multiple streams of income." For example, she says, "Create information products, sell them on the side, and consider affiliate marketing. Make sure your income comes from different sources, because one area of money can dry up."

And if you don't know how to do something — learn. Read, listen, talk, and ask. Or even better, find a few mentors you can trust. Wendy says, "As women, we do not like to ask for help. We don't like to 'not know' the answer, but I simply forced myself to ask." Wendy counts professional bloggers and social media experts, Liz Strauss and Darren Rowse, among the people who can take some of the credit for her success today.

Amanda Steinberg, Founder and CEO • Daily Worth
www.dailyworth.com

Amanda Steinberg is the founder and CEO of Daily Worth, a daily e-mail about finances for women to help them understand money and increase their net worth. Amanda successfully raised $850,000 in venture capital for her company and continues to work from home with her two-year-old daughter and five-year-old son in the mix. Her now 14-person team also works from their homes.

How did she not only raise so much money for her home-based business but also come up with the idea in the first place? Amanda first points to her childhood and the memory of a lot of financial stress as her mom struggled as a single mother.

"My mom really instilled in me the value of creating my own financial independence," says Amanda, who recounts that once in her twenties, she found she was very good at business and making money. "Unfortunately, at the same time I became very good at spending money."

At 30, Amanda examined her finances and realized she had nothing to show for the hard work and high earnings of her twenties, so she began a personal financial journey to learn how to build up her own net worth.

The idea for the basis of her company came after she subscribed to an e-mail called Daily Candy, about fashion. Every day she received an e-mail from the company, and she began to think they had such a smart business model, meaning the structure of how that company generated revenues: Send an e-mail, got a lot of subscribers, sell advertising, make a lot of money with low overhead and expenses. Then Daily Candy sold to Comcast for $120 million.

The idea for Daily Worth was solidified: a daily e-mail aimed at women about personal finances and money management. Amanda had been running Web development agencies for ten years, and started working from home in 2006 when her son was born. She began developing Daily Worth in July 2008, then launched it in January 2009, the same week her daughter was born.

Before actually launching her business, Amanda sought out experts in e-mail companies to be her mentors. She worked diligently on her business model and developed spreadsheets to show how much money she would be able to make against expenses as she grew, and made estimates — projections — out five years. She used her own Web development agency to build the Web site for her new business and found an out-of-work journalist to write content for six months for free, in exchange for four percent ownership in her new company.

It took Amanda nine months to get to 1,000 subscribers, and she realized that the only way to grow big enough to generate significant money would be to get to 25,000 subscribers and beyond. But the only way to do that, Amanda knew, was to have enough money to pay people to help her, and to pay for marketing to attract more subscribers.

After ten years of meeting investors in various settings throughout her career, and then leveraging her vast network, Amanda knew she was willing to give up a percentage of her company to get a $250,000 investment in Daily Worth, so she set out to meet with investors. Getting funded took many months and even more rejections, including one investor who said he didn't think women were even interested in money. Amanda set out to prove him wrong.

With the money she did land from investors — including Eric Schmidt, former CEO of Google — she was able to spend $10,000 a month on marketing and reached 50,000 subscribers. She kept building on her formula for spending to gain more subscribers and was able to raise another $100,000. Daily Worth surpassed 100,000 subscribers, and Amanda hasn't looked back.

While Amanda still works from home, that arrangement isn't always popular with her company's board of directors. She travels twice a week to New York City from outside the city to meet with four of her employees. In between, her team communicates on Instant Message, through e-mail, and by phone many times a day. She believes in her virtual company format.

"We have no distractions, no commute time, and we can be fluid in our lives," says Amanda, who adds that everyone she hires is very results oriented, and she isn't afraid to fire someone who isn't producing. She is also very good at delegating. She knows she can be away at any time and her company keeps running, even during things like a sudden trip to the doctor with her kids.

"The real challenge for women is that they think if they start businesses and people pay attention to them, it will just make money," says Amanda. "I see too many women spending money on marketing, branding, logo design, PR, and they haven't thought through how their business will actually make money."

Amanda admits that the kind of success she is experiencing with her business doesn't come without a price.

"Because I'm so married to my work and my children, it has not been helpful in the area of marriage," she says. She was getting a divorce around the time she landed venture capital, and she is very pragmatic about the pressures of raising this kind of money.

"Once you've raised venture capital, you kind of have a loaded gun to your head," Amanda says. For her, Daily Worth is more than just a company — it's a mission. "I want women to recognize their own worth and value," she says. "I want them to realize market opportunities that exist." She believes that the only thing standing in any of our ways is the limits of our own minds. Don't limit your thinking, she emphasizes.

Go for It

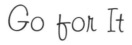

There you have it. Inspiring women who — like you, like us — were moms who were not only determined to be there for their babies or young children, but were also driven to carve out something more for themselves. Their determination and drive puts them on the path toward business success, yet each woman has her own vision of what it means to be successful.

Our experiences are so individual, but there is a common thread that binds us. In addition to being moms or soon-to-be-moms, we have a little fire in our souls. We know there is something simmering just beneath the surface of our roles as chief boo-boo kisser, lunch-maker, bad-dream chaser, and lover of all things about our small people.

You have read this book because you have something calling to you. It may be only a whisper. Or maybe it was a whisper, but now the voice is loud and clear. Our hope is that by hearing our stories and the stories of other moms with home-based businesses, you will recognize parts of yourself. Are you an Alli or a Wendy, constantly reinventing yourself and your career — enjoying each step that allows you to help others? Are you a Selena or an Amanda, driven by a passion in your gut — leading you to combine a business sense with a need to make the world a better place? Are you a Tobi or a Nika, moms who are using the challenges presented by motherhood to reinvent themselves as both moms and business owners? Are you an Aliza or a Danielle, embracing motherhood and passionately exploring new technology for creativity? Our hope is that a lightbulb has gone off as you have read this book — and that the light you see in these pages is one of possibility.

We hope we've given you the motivation you need to put one foot in front of the other and begin your own journey. We have faith in you.

You can find additional resources at the MomIncorporated.com site and interact with us on our Facebook Page (facebook.com/momincorporated) and on Twitter (twitter.com/momincbook). We are excited to say we will also keep you updated on the women in this book and our own progress as moms and business owners, and we'd be happy to profile you, too.

Thank you for being bold enough to join us on this journey. We're excited that you are starting down the path of starting a business. Don't ever get discouraged. Nobody will tell you it's easy. But anyone who has done it or is doing it will tell you it's worth it!

You are Mom, Incorporated. And we're rooting for you!

Our Acknowledgments

We'd like to thank Mr. Ronnie Sellers, the visionary behind the incredible company, Sellers Publishing, who saw a spark in our book idea and said Yes to this book. To our dynamic and ever-patient editor, Mark Chimsky-Lustig, who believed in us and provided more support and inspiration than any author can hope for. To Publishing Director Robin Haywood and the Sellers sales and marketing and publicity team for their enthusiasm, and to Charlotte Cromwell for her amazing production work. Also, a special thanks to Heather Zschock for her beautiful cover and interior design, and to Renee Rooks Cooley and Laura Shelley for their invaluable assistance.

We'd also like to thank author and entrepreneur Carol Roth, for her solid savvy business information peppered throughout this book, and Shannon King Nash, Esq., for her superior consulting on both the legal and taxation sections of this book.

The women who are featured and quoted in this book are a source of inspiration for us. Thank you for sharing your stories, your wisdom, and the heart of your families. You remind us what is possible when you put your mind and soul into the things you love: your dreams and your families.

We found the women featured in this book from a variety of sources, including HARO, Martha Stewart's Dreamers Into Doers, Chain of Daisies, Independent Women's Network, the Mom Incorporated Ning Group, the Mom Incorporated Facebook Page community, Twitter, and some amazing referrals from friends, family, and colleagues. Thanks all.

To Maya Bisineer for sharing her brilliant photographic talent, and taking our author pictures, catching us in a moment of pure joy. We can't look at the book without thinking of you.

Aliza's Acknowledgments

A special thanks to my parents, who have been my biggest cheerleaders all my life and taught me that I could do and be anything.

And a huge heartfelt thanks with hugs to my coauthor and cohort, Danielle Elliott Smith. It has been an absolute pleasure writing with you. We did it!!

Danielle's Acknowledgments

With this being my very first book, I would be remiss if I didn't thank everyone I know . . . from my high school English teacher, Cathy Gibbons, who championed my love of writing, to . . . well, everyone else I've met and loved since then. But, somehow, I don't think that is how it works. So, I will try to be brief.

At the very top of my I-love-you-to-pieces-I-couldn't-have-done-this-without-you list is, naturally, my coauthor, Aliza Sherman. You believed I would be a good addition to this book, and in doing so, have made a dream come true for me. Thank you for your brilliance, your guidance, and good heavens . . . your patience as I learned the ropes. You made this process as peaceful as possible and helped me to believe in my abilities as an author.

A million thank yous to my parents, for teaching me that following my dreams was not only OK, but necessary. From the time I was itty-bitty, Dad's cheerleading and favorite phrase of "OK, Danielle, now here's what you do . . . " and Mom's perfect love and willingness to support my passions have laid the foundation on which I now stand.

To Alli Worthington and Barbara Jones, for being my voices of reason, reminding me what I was capable of, celebrating my successes, and pushing me when I needed it. To Megan Jordan, for being the very first person I read online and a constant source of inspiration. I will always be grateful for your friendship.

To the mentors who can take credit for where I am today: Shelly Kramer, for asking the hard questions, pulling me up onto my feet, and being an example of what it means to love what you do and work hard at it. Stephanie Smirnov, for seeing something in me in 2009 . . . your faith has pushed me to be better. Carol Roth, for your wisdom and advice, and for reminding me to stay true to myself.

To the amazing women I have met since I ventured into this amazing space: Arianne Segerman, Tiffany Romero, Julie Dance, Esther Crawford, Sarah Baldry, Linda Sellers, Molly Teichman, Nirasha Jaganath, Rachel Matthews, and the crew at CA10. Thank you for being the first to cheer with me, as well as the first to pick me up when I need it. I'm grateful to each of you for your willingness to be both friend and sounding board.

My St. Louis online crew — Ria Sharon, Suzanne Tucker, Lisa Bertrand, Kelli Stuart, and Melody Meiners — thank you for your constant encouragement and your hugs. And to my friend Donna Alkire, for the MANY hours you took my small people so I could write, and the MANY, MANY hours you listened to me talk about this writing process. I'm grateful. Sierra Friend — your talent for knowing what I want and need better than I do has translated into two Web sites of which I am extremely proud. Thank you for sharing your immense talents, for your patience when I couldn't put into words what I needed, and for celebrating each moment of joy I have experienced along this path.

Everyone who works at my local Panera on MidRiversMall Drive in St. Peters — not only is your customer service flawless, but you provided me with a "home away from home" that inspired me to work intensely and efficiently toward my goal of completing this book on time.

And finally to my family, Delaney and Cooper — you have been so patient (as patient as two small people can be) with me as I have labored over this book. I am proud of your heart and spirit. Thank you for allowing me to learn how to do both this business I love and to be your Mom. And to my husband, Jeff, for understanding the late nights — giving me a high five at four a.m. as I head to bed and you go to the gym — for doing more than your share of everything family, for picking me up when I needed it, and for forcing me to go back and edit everything I do — you make me better. I am lucky to have someone in my life who believes in me as you do. Thank you. I love you.

Index

Page numbers in *italics* indicate worksheets, checklists, charts, and tips.

About the Authors

Aliza Sherman is a successful serial entrepreneur with over 20 years' experience starting and running companies, particularly on the Internet. She founded the first full-service Internet company, Cybergrrl, Inc., and the first global Internet networking organization for women, Webgrrls International. *Newsweek* named her one of the "50 People Who Matter Most on the Internet." *Fast Company* named her one of the "Most Influential Women in Technology," and she's been included on Forbes.com's "Top 20 Women for Entrepreneurs to Follow," Twitter Grader's "100 Most Powerful Women on Twitter," MyMediaInfo's "Top 10 Twittermoms," and Babble.com's "Top 50 Moms on Twitter." She is the proud mother of five-year-old Noa Grace.

Danielle Elliott Smith is a former award-winning television news anchor and reporter turned blogger, vlogger, video correspondent, media trainer, and public speaker. She is the founder and primary author of ExtraordinaryMommy.com and DanielleSmithMedia.com, as well as the host and producer of Bliss TV. Danielle has emceed events that included guest appearances by First Lady Michelle Obama and Martha Stewart. She has worked as a correspondent at the 2011 ProBowl in Hawaii and at the 2010 Winter Olympic Games on behalf of P&G, and has championed the fight against child hunger, working directly with the ConAgra Foods Foundation. As a result of her work, she has been featured on the *CBS Early Show*, Fox News, MSNBC, NPR, and in *USA Today*, as well as on a variety of Web sites. Danielle has continued to follow her on-camera passion, working the Red Carpet and hosting video events on behalf of the 140 Character Conferences: Exploring the State of Now. She is delighted to be the mom to two small people, her seven-year-old daughter, Delaney, and five-year-old son, Cooper.